KT-500-672

TO11467
Accession Number...... 24.326

Class Number........... 636.142

TRAINING THE
SHOW JUMPER

STEPHEN HADLEY

Compiled and edited by
JUDITH DRAPER

KENILWORTH PRESS

First published in Great Britain 1987 by
Threshold Books, The Kenilworth Press Ltd,
Addington, Buckingham, MK18 2JR

Reprinted 1988, 1992, 1996

© Stephen Hadley 1987

All rights reserved. No part of this publication may be reproduced,
stored in a retrieval system, or transmitted, by any form or by any means,
electronic, mechanical, photocopying, recording or otherwise, without
the written permission of the publisher.

British Library Cataloguing in Publication Data
A catalogue record for this book is available from the British Library.

ISBN 0-901366-74-9

Printed in Great Britain by Hillman Printers (Frome) Ltd

CONTENTS

page

INTRODUCTION

The idea of writing this book was to try to provide answers to all the questions which I am so often asked during training clinics, lectures, and so on. The following chapters are made up from my own experiences with horses and from ideas and information picked up from other people whose opinions I respect, and which, in a small way, have proved successful in my career so far.

I should like to thank the following people, without whose invaluable help the writing of this book would not have been possible: Bridget LeGood, former Editor of *Riding*, whose idea it was that I should one day expand the series of articles which I wrote for that magazine into a book; Peter Jeffery, for his encouragement when he was on the staff of *Riding* Magazine and later for his arduous efforts, in his role as News Editor of *Horse and Hound*, to make a journalist out of me; Judith Draper, for her supreme efforts in the hard slog of getting my written and spoken words ultimately on to the following pages; my parents, for their keen support and interest throughout my show jumping career and for their financial support in the early days; Lars Sederholm, who made the concept of flat work training for the show jumper so much clearer to this largely self-taught rider, and who has helped both my wife and myself for many years; and above all my wife, Clare, not only for her help in the writing of Chapter 11, but also for her unfailing assistance and support in so many ways.

Stephen Hadley

LIST OF ILLUSTRATIONS

CHAPTER 1

Choosing the Right Horse

The price of any commodity is largely governed by the law of supply and demand, and good animals of proven ability are very hard to come by. Show jumping is becoming increasingly popular. Every year new owners come into the game looking for horses either for themselves, for their children or for established riders to travel for them. Since so few animals have the ability to reach the highest level, it is not surprising that the demand for the better horse far exceeds the supply.

Before setting out to look for a show jumper it is of paramount importance to have a plan of campaign. First, consider exactly what it is you hope to achieve and at what level you would like to compete; then decide what type of horse you will need. Naturally your choice will be governed to a large extent by how much money you can afford to spend. Show jumpers come in so many shapes and sizes and from so many different sources that it is impossible to lay down hard and fast rules as to how and where to find the right horse. The ideal would be to buy an animal that you have seen around a little, perhaps at local shows, riding club events, hunter trials and so on. If, after you have watched him in action for a while, you can see that he is genuine, he is the horse to buy – always assuming that the owner will sell.

Never forget that it is far easier to buy than to sell. A little extra time spent looking around will pay dividends. When you do see what you are looking for, and you really feel sure that the horse will suit you, do not delay: buy him before someone else does. If you are not absolutely sure, seek professional advice from a friend or acquaintance whose judgement you can trust, or perhaps from a reputable dealer. Because descriptions of animals can be so misleading, sales are best avoided by the novice horse owner. However, many good horses can be found through advertisements in equestrian magazines. Although you must be prepared to make a few wasted journeys, you will find, on the whole, that horses are for sale for perfectly genuine reasons. Wherever you buy your horse, make sure that he is warranted sound and vice free and that he lives up to his description as far as behaviour is concerned – both in and out of the stable.

The next best thing to buying a made horse is to produce one from scratch. For many years I bought unbroken three-year-olds, mainly from Ireland, and produced them as novices the following season. If they appeared to have the ability to go on, I turned them away to grass for the summer and brought them out again the following winter when the main summer circuit came to an end after the Horse of the Year Show. However, when buying an unbroken horse you have to take into account the expenditure involved in breaking, producing and keeping him until he is ready to compete. Nowadays, because of the ever-mounting expense, I am more inclined to buy a horse who has already shown a little form under saddle. He may cost a fair bit more initially, but often this can be offset by the savings made in not having to bring him to that stage.

The type of horse required is governed to a great extent by the size of the rider. Personally, being of medium height and weighing nearly 11 stone, I have a pretty wide range to choose from. Although the ideal size for a show jumper is about 16.2hh, I would also be keen to buy a smaller horse, even down to 15.3hh or so, if he had plenty of talent. I try to avoid ponderous horses: today there is so much emphasis on speed that a horse has to be really sharp to be consistently successful.

There are many qualities which go to make up a successful show jumper; some are essential, others are luxuries. I feel that of all the ingredients the most important are ability, temperament and conformation.

Ability
It is vital that the horse has enough actual jump. Many years ago, the well-known Yorkshire dealer Trevor Banks said to me that if a horse cannot get a bit of height and width when he is four years old, then he never will. By and large I would agree with that, although there are exceptions, of course. I have had horses who, with schooling, experience and careful handling, have found a little more scope every year right up to Grade A and above.

One perfect example was Flying Wild, the first really good horse I ever had and who won my first important competition back in 1968, the Foxhunter final at Wembley. She was a neat, clean jumper from day one. But, although she won a lot of classes as a novice, several people whose opinions I respect believed that she would always be stuck for distance down a combination or for width across a truly big oxer. In fact, when she came to jump at top level she never really had to struggle to jump anything. She had merely developed a technique which enabled her to jump things which I for one would not have believed possible a year or two before. Unfortunately her career was cut short by unsoundness and she was retired to stud, where she failed to distinguish herself, producing nothing of any note, either as a type or as a show jumper.

In spite of my experience with Flying Wild, however, I really believe that if a horse is to shine at the top level he *must* show above average ability at an early age.

Temperament

However much ability a horse has, he will not make the grade if his temperament does not allow you to make full use of it. An easy-going nature, with an intelligent and generous mind, is the ideal. Show jumpers must be out-and-out triers. They must want to take you to fences and to keep clearing that top rail.

Avoid a horse who is obviously lacking in intelligence. He will never be bright enough to help you in a really tight corner, and is unlikely to be sharp enough to win classes when the pressure is on. At the other end of the scale is the hot, buzzy horse who will rarely let you win a competition of any sort. To win most classes these days you have to turn in really sharp to some fences and even gallop to others from quite a long way out. On regular treatment like that the naturally gassy horse quickly goes over the top and becomes a part-time lunatic.

A good temperament is a tremendous help all round. It is not only the work in the ring which takes its toll on a horse's mind and body but also the training along the way and the travelling, which seems to increase in direct ratio to the horse's improvement. The day-to-day living with a horse is so much easier for both of you if he is basically a nice person, with a brain.

Conformation

As I have said already, jumpers come in all shapes and sizes. If they have sufficient ability, they seem to cope well enough with the odd defect of make and shape. Lack of, or too much size, a lack of bone and substance, and various other disadvantages which at first sight might make you steer well clear of a horse, will not necessarily prevent him from becoming a show jumper – providing he has that explosive feeling when he leaves the ground. But, if a horse

A really good workmanlike sort: he's big enough, strong enough and has plenty of substance which stops just short of being common. Although he's perhaps just a little straight in the shoulder, he'd be hard to fault on any other count and has quality enough for a show jumper. He has a good eye and a tremendous set of limbs. Incidentally, note the 'jumper's bump' (the little hump over the quarters just above the point of the hips), which old horsemen always reckoned denotes a horse with plenty of jumping ability. This one would have a good re-sale value if he didn't make it as a jumper. If he were good across country, he could make an eventer; at the very worst he'd make a high-class hunter, being a superb mover and up to a lot of weight.

is to have a re-sale value in the event of his not making the grade, the nearer he is to the type and size which most people would consider ideal, the more likelihood there is of someone wanting to buy him.

In addition, a quality horse, who is well put together, has a head start because his action and presence will make his training so much simpler than that of a badly made animal. The photographs illustrate a few horses which I would favour as good types.

The head should be well set on to a well formed neck. It is far easier to get a horse bridling corectly if he is narrow around the throat; the horse with a short, stocky or ewe neck will always be more difficult to get 'on the bridle'. A good sloping shoulder suggest that a horse should be a free goer. I dislike a big horse with a pony action. A short-backed horse will always be easier to get into a good riding shape than a long-backed one with poorly made hocks.

Some faults are worse than others. A horse would have to be something really spectacular for me to buy him if he

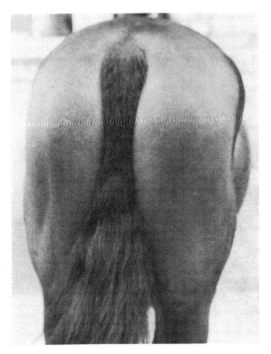

Left: Good hindquarters. When assessing a young potential jumper I look at him first sideways on to get an overall picture. But I soon walk around the back, because that tells me a lot of the things I want to know. A horse's engine is at the rear, and you see few good performers with bad hindquarters. I don't like a horse to be common about his hips. This one has an overall quality and also what I value most of all – a good second thigh (the first muscle above his hocks) which should be well-developed. As in this picture the horse should be marginally wider at that point than at the hips.

Below: A poor back end on an otherwise decent sort of horse. To be fair, he was somewhat light in condition when this photograph was taken, but even carrying 1cwt extra he'd still be a little short of second thigh. In fact, this didn't prevent him from jumping; he had quite a lot of ability and, as his face suggests, was really nice to know. It's always a bonus if you like a horse as well as respect his ability.

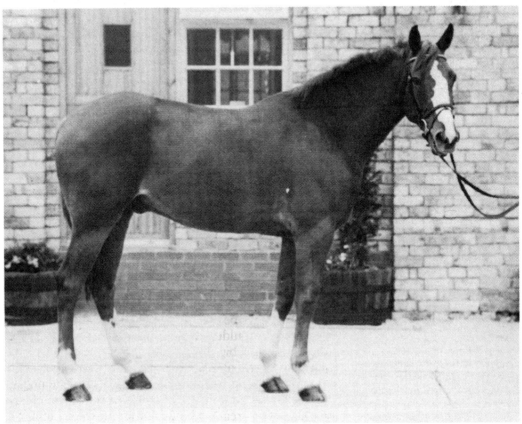

LIBRARY
BURTON COLLEGE
BEVERLEY HU17 8QG

An upside-down or ewe neck. This defect of conformation, in which the muscle in the underside of the neck is more developed than that in the top line, makes life very difficult for a show jumper. It's so much harder to get a horse to bridle correctly if he's made in this way for the simple reason that he's being asked to carry his head in a way that isn't normal for him. This horse came to me as a Grade A, but I'd never buy an untried horse with such conformation. In some cases the fault can be corrected with careful and prolonged work on the flat. A few minutes on the lunge each day with a Chambon or correctly fitted draw reins may also help. But care must be taken with any gadgets such as draw reins. There's no quick way. It's not sufficient to pull a horse's head and neck into the right shape by force alone. What you really need is muscle development in the top of the neck. That only comes, over a period of time, from good feeding and correct work, which in due course puts muscle in the right place. If in doubt, consult an expert.

were badly back at the knee. I can think of few really top-class animals who have had that one basic fault. On the other hand, a horse who is over at the knee rarely goes lame and several good jumpers have been made that way. My old partner, Mr Arnold Clarke's No Reply, was very over at the knee, but had superb, sloping pasterns and excellent feet which served him well throughout his jumping days. It was ironic that his career should have been cut short when he was at the height of his powers by a fused vertebra in his back. The optional operation which he underwent relieved him a little, but he was never the same again, and was retired, successfully, to the hunting field.

Hind legs are another matter and seem to be a law unto themselves. I love clean, sound hocks as much as anyone, but horses with bent, curby hocks can and do win classes at every level. Nevertheless, I can only think that they would have been even better horses, and would have covered the ground in a lot easier manner both for themselves and their riders, had they been better made behind.

Some horses have bad feet, either flat and shelly, which bruise easily, or long, donkey feet, which have little shock-absorbing ability. Horses can jump successfully on feet like that, but the chances are that they would win a lot more and for a lot longer on a really good set of wheels.

Good raw material, with a lot of plus points and just the odd snag (the perfect horse was never born – I certainly never expect to find him). When looking for a young horse one always hopes that his good points will outweigh the bad ones and become dominant in his later life. This horse is a three-year-old bred in Holland. On the credit side he has a lot of ability, as can be seen from his jumping on the lunge in the pictures on pages 14–16. He has also crossed the bridge at which so many horses fail, having kept his jump after a saddle was put on him. He's now making a good shape round a small course. He has a wonderful character, learns fast and will, I'm sure, be successful at whatever level he reaches. He's not very big, being barely 16hh when this picture was taken, and is slightly back at the knee, but he's such a great mover that I'd excuse him that. In fact, the fault is not as bad as this unflattering photograph suggests. He's obviously immature and has a lot of improvement. With normal luck, a horse such as this one would always make a good teenager's/riding club horse if he didn't make the top as a jumper.

Splints never really bother me as long as they are a little way from the knee and not tied in to a tendon. If they have formed and have ceased to be troublesome, just leaving a boney enlargement, they should not prove to be much of a problem.

Testing the Unbroken Horse
I would never buy an unbroken horse without first seeing him pop over a pole on the lunge. Obviously, a horse who shows ability when lunged is still not bound to make the grade. Only a few horses reproduce under saddle what they promise when jumped loose; but I have found that even fewer of those horses who show nothing at all on the lunge become successful show jumpers. It is rather like the pedigree of a racehorse: a horse may be bred to win a Classic and be unable to gallop fast enough to keep himself warm; but if his pedigree is right he will have more chance – at least on paper – than an obscurely bred horse.

When lungeing a horse I would not expect him to jump huge fences; a young horse should never be over-faced. But a good technique is essential. He must be neat in front, and snap his forelegs away in a manner which suggests that he dislikes touching a pole. Avoid the horse who leaves a leg down. He must 'get his shoulders up', bascule and round himself in the air, and show that he has the ability to bend

Opposite, top: It's essential to make everything as easy as possible for the young horse. I'd never come straight to a biggish fence without first giving him a chance to understand what he's doing. I always let a really green horse run through the gap between the wings a couple of times – with no poles at all. Here I've progressed from a pole on the floor to a small sloping pole. The two poles for wings guide the horse to and away from the fence. This youngster is typical of his generation and jumping feet higher than he needs to – not a bad sign! He's looking at the poles and obviously has no intention of touching them, which is also a step in the right direction. He's certainly a bit loose in front in this photograph, but he's going high enough to compensate.

Opposite, bottom: By taking things a step at a time it's easy to keep the horse's confidence and soon have him coming to bigger fences. Again he's dangling in front and at the moment seems more concerned with getting his body out of the way than his front legs.

Above: Most youngsters, when they find out what they're doing, start to take fences with too much pace. Here he's become a little over-bold. The kicked-up shavings show how deep he's run himself in, which in fact helps him to learn how to snap his front legs away. But in fact in this photograph he's not making quite such a good shape because he's run on to his forehand and is not backing off and getting his shoulders high enough. However, that's being hypercritical of a three-year-old who knows nothing.

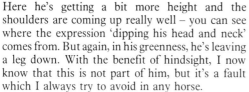

Here he's getting a bit more height and the shoulders are coming up really well – you can see where the expression 'dipping his head and neck' comes from. But again, in his greenness, he's leaving a leg down. With the benefit of hindsight, I now know that this is not part of him, but it's a fault which I always try to avoid in any horse.

Got it right! I think this is a really good photograph, with a great feel of activity about it. He's powered off the ground, is making a super, round shape and is level in front. I also like his expression: he's relaxed but not complacent and is obviously far more at home in his work than he was twenty minutes previously.

his hocks and not be slow behind. He should also give the impression that he is enjoying himself. If he is under pressure and protesting at this stage, his temperament is unlikely to stand the training and stress later in his career.

Bred Right or Wrong

Breeding is of far less importance to a show jumper than it is to a racehorse. Nevertheless a basic knowledge of equine genetics and the history of those sires and bloodlines, both in Britain and abroad, which have stood the test of time and competition, will certainly help you to avoid making mistakes when buying a horse.

The breeding system in Britain is so hit-and-miss as to be hardly worthy of consideration – except perhaps when it comes to a sire who rarely seems to produce anything of note or one who passes on a bad streak of temperament. The progeny of such stallions should, of course, be avoided. Generally speaking it is best to select a horse according to its type, apparent mentality and/or track record, if any.

I do not wish to go into the whys and wherefores of British breeding in this book, except to say that as I see it we have always lagged behind other countries in horse production – and possibly always will – for the simple reason that we do not have (or do not make use of) the right type of indigenous stock. It is bad news for British breeding when so many mares are retired to the paddocks due to unsoundness or insanity – and, believe me, that happens much more often than you might imagine. A little is being done to improve things, through the grading of mares and selection of stallions, by a few dedicated and well-meaning people; but we British are such confirmed individualists that I fear such people will always be in the minority, and will be greatly outnumbered by those breeders who, rightly or wrongly, prefer to go their own way.

Ireland

Among those countries which do have their own good quality breeding stock, Ireland readily comes to mind. The Irish have their traditional draught mares, and there are few crosses in the world to equal the Thoroughbred X Irish Draught. World-famous examples that come to mind include Beethoven, who won the Foxhunter final (incredibly, as a four-year-old) when ridden by his owner, Douglas Bunn, and who went on to win a World Championship partnered by David Broome. Another was Bellevue, for so many years a linchpin of Italian Nations

Cup teams, and a prolific Grand Prix winner for Raimondo d'Inzeo. In fact, in those days the Italians were mounted virtually exclusively on Irish horses. Buttevant Boy, too, came from Ireland as an insignificant looking four-year-old, and grew on to become the strapping 16.2hh winner of Grand Prix at the highest level. My own partner, the aforementioned Flying Wild, was a perfect example of a first cross Thoroughbred/Irish Draught, with her broad, honest face and typical grey colouring. I would buy her, on type, any day of the week.

The Irish have also got it together from a sales point of view. They set out to breed horses for sale, not by mistake. They know what they want to breed, what the buyer is looking for and, in most cases, what it takes to produce a jumper from seed corn. Never make the mistake of thinking that you are dealing with amateurs over there. Horse producing is a major industry in Ireland, and those boys are not tourists. They can produce a horse to perform on the end of a lunge in a way that you would not believe possible, and it is the rule rather than the exception that the horses continue to perform when they are broken.

My one criticism of the Irish system would be the tendency to over-face horse by lungeing them too often over big fences at an early age.

Holland

To my mind the Dutch have really hit the jackpot over the last thirty years or so with their production of the Warmblood, or sporting, horse. They, too, have their own indigenous, country-bred horses whose original purpose was pulling a plough. The ancestors of the modern Dutch horse were developed in Gelderland and Groningen, two quite different areas of Holland where two distinct types of horses evolved. In Gelderland, where the land is light and sandy, a finer type of work horse was needed. In Groningen, a heavy clay area, a heavier, stronger type was bred. Fortunately there was a genetic compatibility between the two breeds. To refine their products Groningen breeders used Gelderlanders, and to add more substance the system was reversed.

Right from the start the farmers always had a policy of weeding out unsuitable animals. Their livelihoods depended on sound horses with good temperaments, and any that did not do the job were culled. With the advent of the tractor the horse population dwindled, but farmers were reluctant to let the horses go altogether and continued to keep a few for breeding. Meanwhile, riding was becoming increasingly popular and riding clubs began to spring up all over the country. Thus arose the need for a true riding horse type. In conjunction with their own old-established bloodlines the Thoroughbred (mainly English) was used extensively, as well as riding horse stallions from France and Germany.

Severe culling has always been, and still is, the focal point of such breeding. It is widely accepted among breeders that that system is the only way to a *perfect* race. If only we had a similar set-up here.

West Germany

Fashions come and go in horses as in anything else, and a decade ago it was the German-bred horse who was in fashion, to the exclusion of most others. The Germans, too, have their own native mares from whom they have evolved a sporting horse which has become one of, if not the most dominating forces in the show jumping arenas of the world. A few generations back the horses were perhaps a little on the hefty side, and occasionally lacking in quality. But selective breeding and the addition of more and more Thoroughbred blood has brought about the necessary refinement, and has combined with the substance and power of the old-type mares to produce horses with power and quality.

In my own experience of German horses, I have found their biggest drawback to be their tendency to require more work, particularly on the flat, and in some cases an inability to remember today what they did yesterday. This is in contrast to the Irish-bred horse, for example, who, having mastered one aspect of training, rarely forgets it.

France

The highly selective French, who have evolved their own Selle Français breed, are to be admired for having produced a uniform, high quality performance horse. I love to study French horses at close quarters in the practice rings of international shows in Europe, particularly in France itself: the two things which stand out above everything else are that the horses literally scream quality and, colour apart, are almost like peas in a pod. They perform, too, and with the present-day emphasis on speed and agility look destined to more than hold their own in the years to come. As a breed, the French horses are perhaps as athletic as any in the world.

Belgium

Like the Dutch, the Belgians produce their own Warm-bloods and are as a result becoming ever more powerful as a show jumping nation. Again, their horses are produced largely from native mares, with the addition of the best blood from other countries, particularly Germany, for the purposes of upgrading.

The Belgians are also making great strides in the marketing of horses, something which is so important to the production line. What incentive is there for breeders if they do not have a good market place? There is little point in striving to produce outstanding animals if at sale time they recoup less than their production costs. No one can run a successful business that way.

Re-Sale Value
Anyone who has a lot of horses through his hands will inevitably also have plenty of failures. I do not think that I am the only person professionally involved with horses who would admit that the majority of animals that come in and out of a yard do not really make it. Of course, it is possible to minimise mistakes by knowing how a horse is bred, by seeing him jump on the lunge, and by utilising every piece of information gleaned along the way to try to assess what type of heart and mind the horse possesses. But, even so, the failure rate is frighteningly high.

For just that reason it is prudent wherever possible to buy a horse who is at least a likeable type and character. Because so few horses make the grade, I always look for an animal who is well put together and who has a good temperament so that, should he not be talented enough to go on to Grade A, he will at least have a 'salvage' value as an eventer, riding club horse or hunter. The plain horse, with a defect of conformation, or one who is a poor mover, would have to be an exceptionally talented jumper for anyone to want to own him. A horse with small, piggy eyes, and with small ears (not a good sign), who is always scowling at the world, will not endear himself to many people. If he then proves to have no talent and, as a result, no place in your stable, he will be very hard indeed to sell on.

Conversely, a well-made, good looking and free-going individual is literally designed to give a rider a nice feel and to be a pleasant conveyance round a show ring or across country. If such a horse is not cut out to be a show jumper, he will more easily find employment in some other related sphere. Many people believe that if a horse has no talent for show jumping, provided he is a good type and a straight mover he is sure to make an eventer. I do not really believe that to be true. A successful eventer needs outstanding natural movement and presence to achieve a high dressage mark, and at least a certain amount of show jumping ability to avoid booting out four fences on the last day. Not many failed show jumpers have all the aforementioned qualities, though if they have some, then they have a headstart. It is those points which need to be taken into consideration when buying a potential jumper. One thing is certain: failed show jumpers quite often make out-standing hunters, so there should always be a job for that class of horse in the hunting field. The only pitfall there is that at the time of writing the price of the average hunter would be perhaps only half the price of the average potential show jumper.

There is no point always looking on the black side, but on the other hand it is important to know what you are letting yourself in for. If you do get a good horse, it should be regarded as a bonus; and if you hit the jackpot by stumbling over a superstar, then that will be a dream come true. It happens to very few people – and lightning rarely strikes the same place twice!

To be saleable a horse must have something going for him. I often find myself telling students that okay, we might not be able to make a good horse out of this one, but if we can at least make him more agreeable to ride, then there will be a job for him somewhere, and somebody will buy him. If a horse is badly mouthed, an uncomfortable ride, has a bad temperament and no jump, it is putting-your-hands-over-your-ears time.

It never ceases to amaze me how so many people go on for so long with totally useless horses. Many of them deserve much better and would be far wiser to cut their losses and get out – even though that might in some cases mean a dramatic hardening of the heart. It is amazing how many riders – particularly girls – become deeply attached to hopeless performers who, apart from having no talent, are in the majority of cases ungenerous hooligans as well.

However, who am I to judge when someone is besotted with a horse and is hell bent on trying to achieve a result that is obviously unattainable? It is their life, and they are entitled to their views. To them all I can say is, in my opinion you deserve better.

Age – When to Start
There is no hard and fast rule about the age at which it is best to start a horse on his jumping career, but of one thing I am certain: bearing in mind how much it costs in time and money – which in a professional yard are one and the same – it certainly pays to find out at the earliest opportunity

just how good a prospect a young horse is.

I prefer to start in the autumn of a horse's third year, mainly because the pressure of the outdoor season is coming to a close; my daily schedule revolves around work in the indoor school rather than the jumping paddock, and I have all winter in front of me to give a horse the time he may need. I do not like to rush horses in the early stages. At that age they are bound to be relatively weak and cannot stand, either physically or mentally, the amount of work which they can in subsequent years.

At this stage it is important to decide whether or not the horse is going to be a long-term prospect. Rightly or wrongly, if I feel that a horse does not have what it takes, I prefer to cut my losses there and then and pass him on to someone else. If he has a lot of other things going for him, with the exception of that all-too-rare out-and-out show jumper's ability, he will almost certainly have a job to do in some less demanding sphere.

But, assuming that his early education has gone smoothly, it is then a good idea to get him going over poles and small fences as soon as possible. Youngsters find plenty of opportunity for a lapse of concentration, and letting them take a look at and pop over poles on the ground, with a little crossed-pole fence a stride or two away, presents no great problem. Again, these early stages must be handled with care and understanding; with the right attitude, and a build-up of confidence, it should not take more than a week or two of patient work to get a horse trotting and/or cantering to small fences. I like to see a little improvement at every session: a little, and often, is best. Never let a young horse become bored or dispirited. There is always tomorrow, and you want him to come out of his box looking forward to his work.

Again, there are the exceptions, but in the vast majority

Before and after

A good illustration of how a young horse can improve given good feeding, work and time to mature. Judy Jones, a rising four-year-old mare, is seen on the right (top) with Tina, having just arrived at my yard: having been badly done as a youngster, she's very weak behind the saddle, with no middle. The bottom photograph, taken two years later, shows the enormous growth potential of horses at that age, especially those from Ireland. She grew a full 3in in little more than two years, though in her case that's only half the story. Had she not been given time to develop mentally, as well as physically, she would never have become the talented performer that she is today. Because she was so weak and backward her early training was unusually difficult. She lived out for most of the first year and was brought in from time to time for short periods of training, then turned away again to develop. Like so many other horses of her age, for a while she completely lost the very considerable jump which I knew she had. After being sold on to Christine Kidner, she was again taken slowly. Ridden by Chrissie herself, she was travelled to shows, given periods of rest and, over about eighteen months, really came back to herself. She's now winning good classes regularly. The moral of this story is, if you're sure that a horse has ability, then sufficient time and good handling will most often pay dividends.

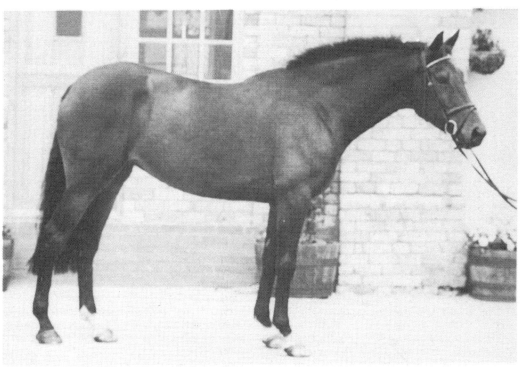

of cases the first few times the horse leaves the ground will give a fair indication of whether or not he has got what it takes. On a horse with real ability the rider does not need anyone to tell him that this one has capabilities worth persevering with. If all goes well, the day will come when you decide that this is the horse you are looking for. That will be enough for the time being. By then you may well be into autumn or early winter, which is an ideal time to rough him off and turn him away for a few months to digest what he has learnt and to grow into a bigger, stronger individual for the following season.

If the winter is fairly open and your supply of grazing permits, it is not unreasonable to allow him to winter out, as long as he is getting well fed morning and night. But, if facilities allow, far better to let him spend his days in the paddock and to bring him in to a good feed and a warm bed at night. That is the method which I prefer. I can see little point in a horse standing with his back to a hedge in freezing rain on a January night if you have an empty stable. But, on the other hand, freedom from education and the demands of human beings can at this stage be of great benefit to his mental and physical wellbeing.

Breaking and Mouthing
Assuming that you have bought a nice type of youngster, probably an unbroken three-year-old, obviously the first job is to get him backed and ridden away, and to put a good mouth on him. Never forget that his early education, good or bad, is more than likely to stay with him for ever.

I have no hard and fast rules about the early education of the potential show jumper and am very flexible where my youngsters are concerned. If I have plenty of staff at the time, it is likely that I will set about the job at home. But if it happened to be a really busy time, I would be quite happy to spend a bit of money having the job done by a specialist with a good record. There are plenty of such people available, who make an excellent job of what is one of the most important parts of a horse's education. Confidence and understanding are everything: through-out a horse's life he must be totally happy and confident in what he is doing. Bad experiences at this stage are to be avoided at all costs. Also, no two horses are the same. Some are easy to handle from the outset and present few problems. Others can be a real headache. If they are not handled professionally, unfortunate situations may arise which will not easily be forgotten.

It is, however, a fact that many horses who prove

difficult in the early stages do very often, with understanding and good training, go on to become top horses later in life. I vividly remember some ten years ago giving £4,400 for an outstanding youngster from Ireland, who threw a tremendous jump on the lunge. He was a 16.2hh three quarter bred and a superb mover. I sent him away to be broken but unfortunately he had a bad experience right at the start. Panicking while being driven in long reins for the first time, he bolted across the school, crashed into the wooden boards and injured himself quite badly. Subsequently he went through two other yards, who also failed to come to terms with him. In desperation I sent him back to Ireland to a yard which had a reputation for succeeding with difficult horses. There he was eventually backed, ridden away and sent hunting for a full season as a fourcoming five-year-old. From then on the story took on a brighter aspect. I had him home – though I found that he was never one that you could leave in the stable for more than a day because he soon became unreasonable again. More than once he fired me into orbit at the start of a morning's work. He still had a big jump, so we persevered and, to cut a long story short, eventually he made Grade B as a jumper, by which time he had become as nice a character as you could wish for. However, he was never quite careful enough to make the top grade and so I sold him on to Maureen Piggott, Lester's daughter, who evented him successfully and in turn sold him abroad, where he continued to compete with the best.

The moral of this story is that it is wrong to condemn a horse too soon, as long as you are sure in your own mind that he does have the ability to do the job for which you want him.

Although that particular horse received his original fright while being long-reined, I am a great believer in having horses driven in long reins at an early age and, if necessary, as part of their schooling in later years. It is truly amazing what results can be achieved by a skilful handler in terms of mouthing a horse and getting him to bend and carry himself.

Whole books have been written on the techniques of breaking horses and obviously that is not what this book is intended to be about – except to say that the importance of these early lessons cannot be underestimated, which is why they are best left to a specialist in the field.

The First Season
As four-year-olds, horses cannot cope either physically or mentally with the same amount of education and work

which they can tolerate the following year. What you do in the first season will very much depend upon the horse and what he tells you he is capable of attaining. A youngster should always be jollied along and have the job made fun for him, although you must at the same time keep a watchful eye on that steady progression towards your intended goal.

The early stages will be spent in going over and consolidating what had been accomplished the previous autumn. Assuming that everything has gone to plan, the young horse should soon be cantering round a very small set of fences. One of the hardest things to achieve with a young horse is a balanced canter at a regulated pace, from which the rider can easily go up or down a gear. For this reason I think it is no bad plan to trot to some fences and canter to others, quite simply as the rider sees fit.

When a satisfactory degree of confidence has been built up round a course including one or two doubles, the time will have come to take him to his first show. Bearing in mind that everything on the showground will be strange to him, it is sometimes a good plan not to compete the first time or two but simply to give him a good look around, and perhaps a little bit of work in a quiet corner and a few jumps over the practice fence, when it is not being used by other riders taking part in a competition. If all goes well, the next time could be the one to ask him to do it for real.

At this stage a clear-round class would be ideal, if possible over a course a hole or two lower than the one he has been coping with confidently at home. After a few such ventures it could well be time for him to take on his first real competition. Choose one of the multitude of minor classes in which riders and producers of young horses now have the opportunity to compete several times a week throughout the summer.

Remember that it is not just the jumping that wears out horses. The long hours of travelling and standing in a lorry can soon make a young horse disenchanted with his job. So keep him fresh and interested at all times. Make a fuss of him. Give him a pat regularly. Let him know that the world is not a bad place to live in. It costs nothing.

Counting the Cost
Having established what is required as far as raw material is concerned, and having discussed a few basic aims, this is perhaps a good moment to examine the situation as a whole. You must be absolutely clear about what you want to achieve in the horse world; how you are going to achieve it, and just what it will cost, not only financially but also in

terms of time, effort and self-sacrifice. Most important of all, can you really justify all that is entailed in the pursuit of a career as a competitive show jumping rider?

I receive numerous requests (some 50 to 100 letters or telephone calls per year) from would-be riders or their parents for advice on how to make a career out of show jumping. No doubt other riders and trainers in the horse world receive similar requests. It goes to show just how many people there are wanting to be involved, compared to how few opportunities exist really to get anywhere. In any sport there is only a small percentage of people at the top who are actually good enough to make a career of their chosen activity. Show jumping is no different. Likewise, in any occupation which provides a pleasant life, cheap labour is always attracted to it. Because so many people are happy merely to be involved with horses, the horse world becomes an employer's market. This is no new subject, but is just the way it is.

From a competitor's point of view, there is no doubt that the top ten or so riders in the country must, in this age of sponsorship and increasing prize money, be earning a comfortable living from the sport. After all, their kind of ability deserves to be well rewarded. But there is a tremendous number of extremely capable people only just below those top riders who are really struggling to earn a living and who must seriously doubt, from year to year, whether it is worth carrying on at all.

Without wishing to sound as if I am throwing cold water for the sake of it, I do feel that readers of this book should be aware of how viable the business really is. Show jumping is a wonderful sport, but from a career point of view it is almost a non-starter – particularly for boys. I honestly believe that unless a boy has indulgent parents, who are able to afford to sponsor him personally, he really ought to make a career in some other sphere so that he will have something to turn back to in case his dreams of becoming a show jumper do not materialise. If his chosen career really takes off, he may then be able to afford to show jump as a hobby. In any case, having put in a five-day week in some other job, he will find plenty of opportunity for competition at weekends.

I well remember having an earnest conversation – as only seventeen-year-olds can – with a pal who is still a great friend to this day. He told me that he wanted only one of two things out of life: either to ride show jumping for a living, or to earn enough money to ride show jumping as a hobby. We went our separate ways, he into computers, myself into horses. Quite recently he and his three partners sold out their by-now extensive company and my friend's personal stake came to £9 million. He now enjoys his show jumping with his own teenage family. The reason for telling this story is that to this day he still thinks that *I* got it right, while I am adamant that *he* did – nobody will ever convince me that on this occasion I am wrong!

There are many examples of people who have done it the right way round – Paul Schockemöhle is just one. As a youngster there was certainly no question of his being able to show jump for a hobby, so instead he set about earning enough to buy his way into horses. Remarkably, and by his own admission, he was not a natural horseman, but through dedication, single-mindedness and dogged hard work he made it right to the top, winning three European Championships in the process. But Paul's success as a rider is exceptional and that is why, rightly or wrongly, I always advise any young man to do something else before trying show jumping. If he does it the other way round and proves me wrong, I would be the first to say well done.

It is not so bad for girls. Perhaps this is a chauvinistic view but, in the vast majority of cases, within a decade they are going to be somebody else's responsibility. So if they are happy enough to take on the hard slog and long hours, then there are a lot worse ways of earning a living. The girl who tells everyone that she wants to become a show jumper will rarely succeed. However, if she is happy to set her sights a lot lower – perhaps working in a show jumping yard and, if she is lucky, travelling to shows as well – she will broaden her experience and, if she is a competent rider, will at least ride good horses at exercise. If she is skilful and sympathetic enough, she will have every chance of helping to school some of the horses in their flat work. If things go well, she might even be rewarded with a few rides in public on young horses. Lucy Collins is one example of that way through. She worked weekends and after school for Ann Fenwick, now Mrs Harvey Wilson and living in New Zealand. After Ann's departure Lucy took over riding novice horses for Ann's father, Raymond, which she does to this day with conspicuous success.

Although show jumping riders come from all walks of life, it does seem that those from a farming background, with a leaning towards horses, stand the best chance of success. They have, after all, built-in facilities: land, stables and forage. David Broome, Liz and Ted Edgar, Rowland Fernyhough and Tony Newbery all came in that way. Yorkshire is renowned for producing gritty sportsmen who climb to the top from small beginnings, Harvey

Smith, Malcolm Pyrah and John and Michael Whitaker being prime examples. They all came from grass-roots beginnings but they all had one common denominator: talent. They would have succeeded in any age.

Nowadays in the late 1980s nothing is guaranteed. Gainful employment is not easy to come by, even if you are well qualified. If you fail to make it in horses, just what do you turn your hand to five years later with no other trade or profession?

Having got all that off my chest, I shall climb down from my soapbox and for those of you who are still with me and still determined to pursue an interest in horses, I will get down to the business of how to train the show jumper.

The following chapters are made up of personal observation and experience, and valuable advice from other people which, in a small way, has worked for me personally. Different people have different ideas and methods. I believe wherever possible in steering a middle-of-the-road course and, above all, in trying to keep everything simple.

CHAPTER 2

The Rider's Position

The rider needs to be in a good workmanlike position, but above all he needs to feel at ease and comfortable in the saddle. The self-taught or semi-educated rider will for the most part be comfortable, but will he be effective? It is surprising how many of those people with whom I become involved in training-clinics, both at home and away, ride with the knee firmly against the saddle and the heel and lower inside leg away from the horse's sides. It may work, or has worked, for them to a degree. But after a few minor changes of leg position there is always a radical improvement in the seat, the rider's control and the performance of the horse. I am not saying that their old position is wrong – not entirely anyway. A novice rider may feel more secure by 'gripping with the knees', and in any case I was one of many who took that as gospel from childhood. However, times change and experience usually improves performance.

To a degree, the dressage seat has similarities to this knee-on, heel-away syndrome. But I believe that the all-round rider can obtain a more driving, secure seat by having the knee slightly away from the saddle so that it allows the heel to come into contact with the horse's side all the time. This is the way to achieve control over the horse: having the heel close to the side so that it is there either to support, maintain or increase the impulsion. How many times do you see a rider break from canter into trot and have to resort to a kick to get the horse cantering again when, if the heel had been in contact with the horse's side, he would have maintained the forward movement? The rider would then have felt the slackening in the rhythm and could have applied pressure from the leg to ensure that the horse did not fall back into trot.

The heels are without doubt the driving force. The rest of the body should remain tall, quiet and elegant, with an almost total lack of unnecessary movement or rocking about: rather, it should be strong and still. The hands should be carried slightly in front of the rider and above the withers with, at all times during work, a contact with the horse's mouth. Here, again, I would diverge slightly

Good leg position at rest

There's much in this picture worth discussing. The heel and lower inside leg (inner calf) are where they should be: well down and around the sides of the horse. The boot sole is clearly visible and, when viewed from above, just the tip of the toe is visible in front of the knee. There's a feeling of closeness about the whole leg, not only because of the obviously firm, reassuring contact of the lower leg, but also right from the heel up through the inner thigh to the seat, which has a lot of depth, with the riding sitting right in the middle of the horse. From this position a rider looks to have his legs 'half way through the horse' if necessary.

The knee is away from the saddle, which is not a problem. Like so many children, I was taught to grip with the knees: wrong! It achieves nothing except perhaps as an aid to not falling off, but there are other methods of preventing that. One has only to look at the thickness of leather and padding at knee level to see that pressure exerted there will have little benefit. It's one of the most insensitive areas of the horse's sides, too.

Thanks largely to the position of the knee, the seat bones are open and deep. Perhaps to be very critical, I'd have the thigh just a fraction further forward, but all in all the rider is no doubt supremely comfortable with a seat like that and is in the best possible position to deal with any situation. The hands are soft and relaxed; the little finger looks poised to slip over that rein when the rider decides to take up the rein again and go back to work.

This picture also illustrates what I've found works best as far as saddles, numnahs, etc, are concerned. I use a thin quilted numnah, either shaped like the saddle or square, always white for appearance, but easily washable. Just as important is a foam rubber back pad, which goes no further down the sides than shown here. This gives the horse's back all the protection it needs from the considerable downward force of a deep seat and a substantial European saddle, but at the same time it avoids further bulk under the rider's leg, where he least needs it. As to the saddle itself, I now use a Stubben Danloux jumping model, partly because I really like their shape: they encourage the rider to sit deep into them, which is so valuable when one's working with pupils. Also, they're good sellers second hand. I try to avoid having saddles that are more than two years old (one day you find yourself with a tackroom full of geriatric saddles). This one has all the features I like: a cut-back head for freedom and comfort at the wither; a deep seat with a high cantle for comfort and security of seat; a wide knee roll with a suede knee, and a block behind the

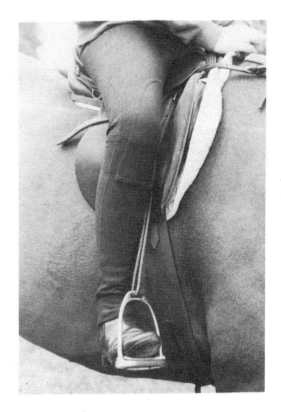

thigh to help keep that lower leg where it should be. I like to tuck the end of the stirrup leather away through the loop provided because I hate any clutter under the leg. The leathers are of soft but very strong rawhide or buffalo.

At the withers it's just possible to see the back pad, fitted well forward to protect that sensitive area which again gets a lot of downward pressure. The white numnah must have a cord, which fits around the lower panel of the saddle as shown here, otherwise it has an annoying habit of working its way backwards and sometimes departing altogether. This horse needs a breastplate to stop the saddle slipping back. I prefer this leather type to the one designed like a horizontal girth, which I always feel tends to cut off the horse's air supply.

Stirrups should be plenty big enough to allow easy access and departure for the foot, and a rubber stirrup tread as shown is a must. This one has seen some action and is quite worn down.

I tend to use the best saddles at all times, but use old bridles at home for exercise, and old girths such as the one here, which is a soft washable lampwick that's comfortable for the horse. It means that the show girths don't have to be cleaned every day.

LIBRARY
BISHOP BURTON COLLEGE
BEVERLEY HU17 8QG

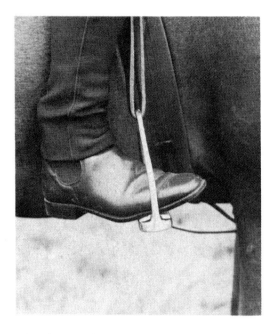 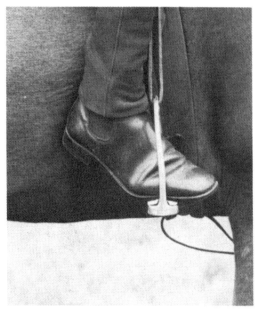

This close up shows the lower part of the leg in a good working position. The heel is well placed, ready to be used inwards and upwards to push the horse into an upwards and forwards movement. Spurs are an optional extra. Some riders wear them as a matter of course; I only wear them on horses who need sharpening up a bit. There are no end of varieties of spurs on the market and it's best to have several different pairs to suit different needs.

The horse is asked to go forward by raising the heel and squeezing. The pucker of skin shows the direction in which the heel asks for the movement. Note the upward lift given by the rider; later on, a similar movement at the point of take-off persuades a horse to pull out another inch or two of height and width over a fence. The heel is being used to maximum effect and is about to be lowered again in readiness for another aid.

from what is sometimes accepted as the norm. Allow the hands to move and be independent. In a dressage test this may not be approved of, but I cannot see any reason for sitting in 'the correct position' and never allowing yourself to move your arms and aid the movement and direction of the horse.

Use of the Leg

The legs should be supple and should form a light 'frame' around the horse – not gripping, but in light contact. In this way they are ready to give whatever aid is needed. They may be used merely as a support – for instance, an outside leg on a corner, used to stop a horse drifting – or as a direction – to maintain impulsion or to strike off in canter using the inside leg. The rider should be able to move his legs independently of his body without disturbing the position of the upper body. If the leg is too far forward, it will reduce the effectiveness of the rider's seat, weakening

Here the lower leg is too far back and well behind the vertical. Although the heel is in contact, it can't be used to good effect from there. The knee is pitched forward and on to the saddle and the rider is perching on the saddle rather than sitting deeply into it. This is a totally ineffective position; the rider has no security in the saddle and is in a bad position either to make any contribution to the job in hand or to cope with an unexpected action from the horse.

Gripping with the knees. There's no way that the rider can achieve a truly deep seat since the grip gradually pushes the seat out of the saddle. The lower leg is nowhere near the horse's side and at this moment is doing nothing. When a leg aid is required, the rider will resort to a kick. The horse can't move in a consistent way since the aids will be neither constant nor always apparent.

A good exercise after first mounting. Lift both legs away from the saddle and upwards to open the seat bones and settle the seat deeply into the middle of the saddle. Then kick the legs down as if you want to get rid of your boots. It's remarkable how much more depth this will give your seat. It's also a good exercise to use every so often in everyday riding in order to check up on your seat and leg positions.

the back aids and possibly causing the rider to haul on the horse's mouth as a means of support. If the lower leg is too far back, it will cause the rider to perch on the saddle and to balance on the knee, again not a good driving position.

The rider should be able to feel the horse in front of him. He should feel in command of any given situation and be able to adapt his position around the basic outline as necessary; he should have a sense of power and the feeling that when he wants to execute a particular movement the horse will respond to the well-applied aid.

The Hands and Arms

The hands should be held directly in front of the rider a little above the withers and should maintain a light, even contact on the reins. The upper arms should be parallel to the rider's sides at rest, the forearm maintaining the accepted straight line from the elbow, through the forearm, wrist and rein to the horse's mouth. The arm should be able to move as one with the reins, thus maintaining an even contact without unnecessary shortening and lengthening of the reins. A rider should never be afraid to move his arms, or indeed his whole body, in an uninhibited way as long as it is done fluidly and tidily and with maximum effect on the horse's obedience and performance. A stiff, rigid rider in the so-called correct position, never daring to move out of it, will surely transmit that stiffness to the horse.

Work Without Stirrups

Work on the flat without stirrups is a great help in all basic exercises. It creates a deeper seat and an ease of balance in the saddle. A secure seat will in turn give the rider the confidence to tackle anything he wishes. Work without stirrups is also beneficial as a means of checking and re-checking the rider's position. A round-shouldered, stiff rider will bounce about while trotting, no matter how smooth the horse's action. If you find yourself bouncing, take your legs right away from the horse's sides to open the seat bones and enable you to come closer to the saddle. Above all do not be tempted to grip with the knees as this will only make you bounce up and off the saddle. Most important of all, relax. Do not be afraid to hold the pommel of the saddle for a few strides. It will certainly help you to relax, lessen your resistance to the action of the horse and start you off in the correct way.

On the Lunge

To stress the importance of arm and shoulder movement and to alter and improve the position of the legs, when teaching at home I very often start people on the lunge. My wife, Clare, excels at improving riders on the lunge and consequently always gets the job in our firm. At some point during their tuition many pupils benefit from a lunge lesson or two, to tighten up certain areas and to make them

Opposite, top: Working without stirrups is time well spent, for it deepens and establishes the rider's seat. The leg should be long and relaxed, lying around the side of the horse, with the heel down and toe slightly raised, as shown in the photograph on page 31. The legs-away-from-the-saddle exercise is invaluable for giving more depth to the seat. Tension makes the rider insecure, so if you find that you have a tendency to bounce around in the saddle, take your legs away from the saddle altogether for a stride or two: it will help remove tension and prevent any tendency to cling.

Opposite, bottom: A good working picture of both horse and rider. The rider's position is sound and the rein contact good, with a straight line from the elbow to the bit. This work can only be beneficial for both horse and rider, since it's deepening the rider's seat and getting the horse to bend and flex from close seat and leg contact.

In this photograph the rider is relaxed and in a good position. The general outline gives me the feeling that everything is under control and that the horse, too, is relaxed and concentrating on the work in hand. The rein is supportive but soft. Note the relaxed hold on both reins. The horse is accepting the situation completely and is reaching for the ground to go long and low. His hocks are well underneath him and the whole top line is working. Note the split in the muscles of the neck.

more aware of how their body works on a horse, what control it has, and how to achieve it. But the bottom line really is to establish a strong, sound leg position.

We lunge the rider with the stirrups much shorter than normal and with no reins. The horse wears a loose pair of draw reins, which gently 'advise' him to carry himself correctly. The principle is that the rider will learn to use his leg in such a way that the horse goes forward in a good shape without the rider using the reins. The short length of stirrup makes it difficult for the rider to grip with the knee, and at the same time ensures that the heel comes into contact with the horse and is always there to maintain or increase the impulsion.

Performing the exercises without reins makes the rider very much aware of how the shoulders and back can work and become more effective when he does have reins again. It is possible to slow or stop a horse on the lunge without reins just by using the seat and back in the correct manner: that is, a straight back, square shoulders and leg directly underneath the seat, and sitting 'against' the horse as opposed to riding him forward. It is important not to sit forward or behind the vertical, as this will cause the effect to be lost. The lunge lesson is an ideal way of making the rider aware of the power his body has over the horse when it is used correctly.

Here the rider looks very apprehensive. Due to ill health on the part of our original 'guinea pig', Charlotte stepped in to the lunge lesson pictures at the eleventh hour. I'd never actually seen her on a horse and she'd never had a lunge lesson. It was quite an ordeal for her to have a photographer present throughout the session. Note the short length of stirrup; the upper body tall; the hands on the hips, thumb towards the small of the back; the heel well down (flexion of the heel improves with practice); the knee loosely on the saddle – with daylight between you and the saddle it'll be easier to stay in balance. There's a good bend to the knee and the heel is underneath. The weight should be in the heel unless the latter is being used upwards.

At walk the horse is being moved forward from an upward lifting heel. Charlotte hasn't quite grasped bringing the knee away so that the heel comes into close contact with the horse's side at all times – but at least she's smiling now.

Still at walk. Here the leg position is better. The rider must learn to maintain the leg position and use the legs while doing other things with her arms and upper body. With her arms held out in front of her she becomes aware, because of the extent to which the arms float about, of how much movement there is in the whole of the upper body. She can learn how to adjust her body and to use the joints to keep the arms level.

Each part of the body should be able to move independently of another. Here the rider is circling the inside hand backwards. As the hand passes the rider's head, the knees are rolled away from the saddle to open the seat bones and sit the rider more deeply into the saddle. The body should be taller and straighter. Whatever the rider does with her hands the body shouldn't alter its position to compensate.

Moving into sitting trot. The rider should always be allowed to hold the pommel with the outside hand to lend security to the seat. There's little point in not holding on and then bouncing around, since the idea of the lunge lesson is to deepen the seat and make the rider feel more secure. In this photograph the rider's looking down and isn't sufficiently relaxed.

Rising trot, with both hands on the hips. This is difficult to do at first as the rider's original balance has been destroyed and she'll be more conscious of the effect of her leg position on her seat in the saddle. Here Charlotte's seat is in the saddle and her heel is down. I'd expect her heel to be pushed further down as she rises. Gradually she should become accustomed to closing her heel on the horse's side in an upwards movement as she sits, and pushing it down to its maximum depth as she rises. Thus, each time the horse takes a stride he's asked to move forward, or at least to maintain his pace. Again in this picture the rider lacks confidence and is still looking down.

Standing at the trot, an exercise which tests and improves the rider's balance. To maintain this position there must be plenty of flexion in the ankle and knee joints and the rider mustn't rest on the knee but should try to keep daylight between the leg and the saddle. The rider should appear to be a frame around the horse until the heel is reached.

Here the rider has taken her hands away from the horse's neck to test her balance. This photograph has caught her resting on her knee – I would prefer her to have less knee pressure and to have her leg more underneath her in order to aid the balance.

Strike-off into canter. If the rider is a little insecure, it's best to strike off while holding on with the outside hand (always use the outside hand so that the rider follows the direction of the circle). The aids are the same as for a normal strike-off. On the lunge the rider has an opportunity to concentrate on keeping the upper body still and letting the canter come from the upward-lifting heel. If the heel is used inwards and upwards, the horse will be lighter in his canter than if he's been kicked forwards, which will leave him rather flat and long.

The canter becoming more established. The rider appears to have just used the heel upwards. Ideally the heel should be used at every stride of the canter to improve and maintain the impulsion. The knee is still tending to grip and the rider is collapsing the inside hip. But for a first attempt it's not bad.

The rider in standing canter position. It's a good idea to alternate between sitting and standing in order to improve the rider's balance and to adjust the lower leg position. Charlotte still needs to bring her knee more away. Riders generally need three or more lunge lessons to adjust their original seat and correct any bad habits.

Here Charlotte is taking an imaginary half-halt, exaggeratedly taking a check 'around' the body. This has a great effect on the whole body, through the opening of the shoulder blades, the separating of the hands and the elbows passing the hips. For maximum effect the leg must be directly underneath the hip and shoulder. The upper body should be tall and elegant. The rider can perform downward transitions by pushing down through the seat bones. Going one step further, by 'taking a check' the rider will be able to stop the horse without reins. The essence of the lunge lesson is the control the rider acquires, through the seat and legs, over the horse's movement up and down through the gears.

A congratulatory pat from the saddle. Always reward the horse during and at the end of a work session so that you stay on good terms with your horse and make him realise that he's doing well.

Here the horse is working well but the raised position of the rider's hand suggests that she's trying to 'shake him loose'. He may have become heavy and be taking advantage of the fact that he's carrying his face behind the vertical.

Another way to 'shake loose' or test that the head carriage and bend are not 'hand held' but are being maintained by the leg position and forward riding. Ride the horse forward positively from the leg into the outside hand, and on a bend, or in places through a circle, pass the horse the inside rein. If he maintains his shape then he's being ridden from the leg and not in a fabricated shape. This can also be done with both hands, in such a way as not to cause a loop in the rein, but to pass the horse through to a long and low position. The exercise shown in the photograph can be used on a strong horse who leans, or one who simply prefers to travel on his forehand. The action of giving the rein or reins stops the horse becoming dependent upon the rider for keeping his head off the floor.

Taking the horse around the inside leg. The stirrup leather is slightly in front of the vertical, although the leg isn't too far forward. The rider's leg position needs adjusting, with more weight in the heel. The hand's coming around the body, i.e. towards the hip not the stomach, so that the horse's nose comes into the bend or circle and the bend comes around the rider's leg and through the horse's body from poll to tail. Note the support with the outside hand and good soft contact to the inside.

CHAPTER 3

Ground Work and Basics

As in any profession, the day always seems to swing along better if working conditions are good and the environment a happy one. That applies as much to a horse as it does to a human. It is essential for horse and rider to be on good terms with each other, and before beginning a schooling session the rider should plan what he hopes to achieve that particular day.

It rarely pays to work a horse to the point of near exhaustion; what cannot be achieved in one day is best left to the next. Usually an hour or so is plenty for one session. On odd occasions a horse may really need to 'work through' a problem, and at this point it is justifiable to work a little longer to get the message home. But the rider must always be on the lookout for the point where the horse is about to go over the top – from then on, work can only be detrimental. I like a horse to go back to his box with a smile on his face. The next day he will start fresh, and progress will continue. But always give him a few minutes easy exercise first: a walk about on a longish rein, and a nice relaxed trot around the paddock before you ask him to come to order again, does a lot for his morale.

I have always felt that when dealing with a young horse the most difficult thing about show jumping is not the actual jump itself but getting from one fence to the other. If a horse has ability and is bold enough, handling the jumping side of things is largely down to him. Getting him to the fence balanced, collected, with the right amount of impulsion and from a good stride (take-off) is the rider's job.

It follows that there are various areas of training on which to concentrate. The main ones are starting, stopping, the bends and changes of direction, and transitions, both upwards and downwards, including half-halts. When schooling, the rider must force himself to work on the things at which he or his horse does not excel. It is such a temptation in a schooling session to run enjoyably through a series of exercises at which the horse is already quite competent, and to avoid movements which he finds

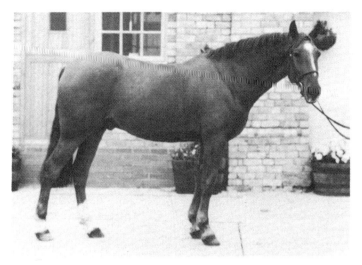

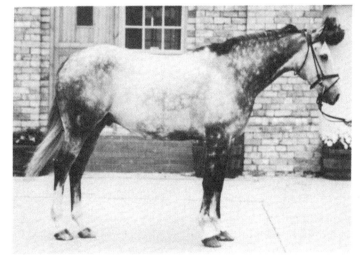

To illustrate this section I've used Eilberg (top) and Russell (bottom). Eilberg is named after the well-known German dressage trainer, Ferdi Eilberg, now based in this country. Ferdi told me that he had a horse who wasn't suitable for dressage but who had a jump in him. He was right on both counts. Eilberg, a chestnut gelding standing about 16.1hh, was a seven-year-old when these photographs were taken. He's first cross Hanoverian/Thoroughbred and, as you can see, a really good sort. Although he's a sweet horse in the stable he's a tough customer to ride and as hard as nails. At the time of writing he'd won a few novice competitions and I think he's worth going on with, as he has a big jump. If I can channel his mind and body in the right direction, he should become a decent show jumper one day. Russell, who is a great mover on the flat, turned out not to have the same talent for jumping and has been sold on (see Chapter 7).

difficult. But, if the difficult points are not practised at home, they will certainly be magnified under the pressure of competition.

It is not difficult to compare a schooling session on the flat at home with jumping a round in a competition. To negotiate a course of fences requires a number of changes of rein (the bends) and a check if the horse is approaching a fence on a wrong stride (the equivalent of the half-halt on the flat). That a horse must be obedient to the hand and heel goes without saying, for not only must he be able to shorten his stride in answer to a check, he must also be able to lengthen it when moved towards a fence. So you need to have the same attention to detail in your approach to a flat-work session at home as you would give to a round in a competition.

The relaxed walk

Opposite, top: This is Eilberg's natural way of going: he likes to amble along with his head in one county and his hocks in the next. For a quality horse he can be a tank to ride, especially during the first few minutes of each session, until he's worked through. Like most German-bred horses he needs plenty of work and constant reminders of how things should be done. However, this photograph is a good illustration of how a horse should begin each session. He's ambling along with a relaxed, happy expression and a nice swing to his tail. He's covering a lot of ground with his stride. After work, and during any breaks, it's a good thing to let a horse walk about on a loose rein so that he can relax, though he shouldn't be as sloppy as Eilberg is here. A horse should always go home on a good note.

Opposite, bottom: This is an improvement. The outline's a little shorter and there's more activity in the hind legs. Clare's obviously giving and taking with the reins and moving the bit through the horse's mouth to lighten the forehand, using the heel of the inside leg in an upwards position. She's softly pushing the middle section away and the inside hind leg as far under as possible, thus transferring the power from the inside hind leg to the outside (left) hand. This hand controls the pace, while the inside (right) hand controls the direction. The outside leg prevents the horse from drifting sideways or off a true line. Because Eilberg's extremely heavy, and difficult to hold together, he has to be continually bullied and cajoled to achieve and maintain a good shape but, as his eye and ears suggest, he stands for it very well. It was a temptation to use an easier horse as a model, but I settled for Eilberg because I feel that he's the embodiment of nearly all the problems that riders encounter with their flat work. This photograph perhaps catches the inside hand a little guarded and near the withers. However, closer inspection reveals that the rein isn't against the neck, which would create neck reining and would only achieve a bend from the withers forward as opposed to one from head to tail. It's always best to have a bend throughout the full length of the horse, around the rider's inside leg, with the inside hand taking the bend by coming around the rider's body.

Above: This is a little better still, but Eilberg's nose should be a bit closer to the floor. He is, I hope, about to be offered a little more rein. Clare's right hand should be a little higher and out of that restricted area. Despite these faults, the actual walk is good; the horse is going somewhere and, again, covering plenty of ground with that front leg.

It cannot be stressed enough how important the flat work is, particularly to the novice. Even if he is not blessed with the greatest talent, he can cope with the fences in Newcomers and Foxhunter classes adequately enough. If you can make him balanced, supple and obedient on the flat, you will find this very beneficial to his jumping.

The horse must go where you point him, and must start and stop when you ask him. In any course of eight fences there are sixteen transitions: eight upwards and eight downwards. You ask the horse to go forward and take on a fence eight times, and conversely, on landing you ask him to come back to you again and to shorten eight times. You also have to cope with at least four or five changes of direction, so it is essential that the horse co-operates with the rider at all times.

I do a lot of teaching, and if I had to choose possibly the most common fault of all amongst novice riders, it would be that they rarely have the engine going. The horse is a rear-engined animal: all the power comes from the hind legs. This must be controlled between the rider's legs, seat and hands, so that it can be drawn on when required. The movement must always come from the back to the front, not from the front to the back. There is no point in trying to pull a horse into a good shape without the hocks operating correctly first. Once the horse is going correctly forward, with a nice bit of life to the stride, it is much easier to work on the front end and to make the horse carry himself properly.

I always try to explain by saying, 'put the two ends together and get the middle to come up'. Imagine that you are holding a stick with both hands, one at each end, and then by turning the hands downwards you shorten the length of the stick. What happens? The middle comes up. When you turn your right hand over, imagine that you are putting the hocks underneath the horse; the turning down of the left hand represents the horse giving in his jaw and arching his neck, while the middle of the stick bending upwards represents the horse raising his shoulders, and the withers actually growing an inch or two, just by the very fact that you have shortened his outline. With the horse now carrying himself, he becomes light on the forehand; as a result he will find jumping much easier, because his front end is virtually part way off the ground already.

Imagine a jet taking off. When it has reached maximum speed down the runway, because there is so much power coming from behind it only needs just the faintest touch on the stick to become airborne, the front end having become

The Trot
The horse has just been asked to go into trot. The rein contact, soft at first, encourages him to think forward and to go in a straight line. Eilberg, however, has immediately reverted to his favourite shape.

There's a lot more collection now, though still from a soft hand. The horse isn't being held in a shape by force; the shape has come from the leg aids and light contact. He's now ready to start working harder and to go long and low, which will build up his outline. Compared with dressage and show horses, he's overbent, but show jumping is a different game altogether and demands that a horse operates best from a round stride rather than a long one. Work in a short outline and with pressure on the horse's top line will build up muscle in the right places, so that eventually he'll find it easier to go that way. I don't agree with the minority of riders who pull a horse into shape by force, usually with the aid of draw reins. That's a short-term means to an end, not an end in itself. The unfortunate animal usually puts his head in the wrong place again as soon as the draw reins are removed. It's no use training a horse by artificial means if you can't achieve the same result in the ring without the gadgets.

Eilberg's working nicely, but care needs to be taken that he doesn't lean on the hand. As I know the horse so well, I can sense that he's about to try to fall on to his forehand again. However, Clare is aware of the situation and is pushing him with her heel while supporting the outside shoulder with her left hand. The inside hand is spot on: light and soft but with a guiding contact. The stride is good – he can really do it so easily.

Nice soft work on a bend: the horse is being led around the inside leg by the rider's inside hand (which is perhaps a little restricted) while the outside hand still supports the outside shoulder. The rider is in the sitting phase of rising trot. The heel is on the horse's side to maintain impulsion. Note that the rider applies the leg as the inside hind leg meets the ground.

so light. A Grand Prix racing car has spoilers on it literally to keep it on the ground – an exaggeration, perhaps, but nevertheless apposite.

If you can get a horse to come lightly off the ground in front, in a good shape, and at the same time thinking and going forward, that really is half the battle. The horse needs to be absolutely level in his paces, not alternately on and off the bridle. So many horses are always running against the hand, as if they are running away from something, which in effect they are. They are running away from a situation which they neither like nor understand. The majority of horses who rush fences only do so because they want to get their jumping over and done with as soon as possible.

The other extreme is the horse who breaks into a trot or pulls up altogether when you ask him to shorten his outline or take a check on the way to a fence. That is the horse who is not accepting the leg, as a result of which he cannot be in a good enough shape to do himself justice. Nor can he accept the rider's advice well enough to enjoy a smooth passage round a set of fences.

Pace and Impulsion – A World of Difference
A worried horse will often gallop recklessly into fences, which can only mean that he wants to get his jumping over with as quickly as possible. Likewise, many novice riders tend to have far too much pace, in the mistaken belief that enough sheer speed will cover a multitude of sins. It is just not so. Impulsion is needed all the time. As I said earlier, you must have your horse going somewhere, but he must be going to fences on your terms, not his. Since a horse has no idea of how much or little speed is required to jump any particular fence, it follows that his rider must develop his own feeling for rhythm, pace and impulsion.

If a horse is established in his pace and accepts implicitly the use of the hand and heel, it is a simple matter for the rider to increase pace merely by opening his hand and letting out a little more of the contained power, put there from the hocks via a sound seat and leg position. You do not see top riders blazing into Grand Prix fences from six to eight strides away, with their horses as flat as pancakes. The exact opposite is the case.

A level pace is essential – neither too much on nor too much off the bridle. The horse should be totally relaxed, with the rider dictating the pace. Only experience will teach you the ideal pace for each and every fence. If in doubt, ask yourself the following questions. Is the horse going on your terms? Are you capable of stabilising his

Work at canter

The best way to lighten a strong horse, or one who's heavy in the hand at canter, is to bring the seat out of the saddle and shorten the reins. Rest the inside hand on the wither and with each successive stride use the heel of the inside leg continually to build impulsion. Again the outside hand controls the pace.

The horse gradually rounds his neck and lowers his head. The rider is asking the middle to come up and, by keeping the seat out of the saddle, allows it to do so, so that the roundness of the stride increases. As the horse relaxes, the hand no longer needs to rest on the wither, something which is only employed to restrict the length of rein in which the horse has to fit himself.

The seat should stay out of the saddle until the horse has really relaxed, when he should be able to maintain the canter shape with the seat in the saddle.

This exercise may be used to sharpen up the canter and to lengthen and shorten the stride. The horse learns to accelerate and move away from the leg in a good shape. Taking it a stage further, the rider may sit for shortening and stand for lengthening, allowing the horse to 'grow' underneath him.

Russell showing a good relaxed canter. His canter tends to be a little impetuous, as if the hindquarters are overtaking the front. This has been eradicated by cantering serpentines of at least six loops down the length of the school, each time changing the rein by halting over the centre line and striking off from halt on to a change of leg. After only a few loops an impetuous horse starts to become more rideable. After five to ten minutes of this exercise, ridden in a quiet, relaxed manner, he'll have improved a good deal. Halt, strike off and balance of canter are all included within this one exercise, after which you could progress to further canter work.

pace? And are you confident that you are working with true impulsion, not merely papering over the cracks with sheer pace alone?

Transitions

To go up or down a gear, the horse must be in a good position and in the right frame of mind. As I see it, there are many parallels between riding a horse and driving a car, especially where the distribution of power is concerned. I am told that any advanced driving instructor will advise you to brake into a corner and drive out of it. The same applies to a horse – he must always come out of a corner going somewhere, but most of all going where you point him. There are many situations in the ring where a rider has to make instant decisions, has to shorten or lengthen and to change direction with split-second timing, particularly when going against the clock. It simply will not do for a horse to be so slow to react that he takes two or three strides more than he should to go from the leg or to shorten to the hand between fences. Lengthening and shortening need to be perfected at home. If a horse will not respond to the aids in basic flat work, he certainly will not when faced with a course of fences.

Starting and stopping
It doesn't always work! This is a pretty awful halt. The horse has thrown his head up in an effort to evade the bit; the rider's body has slipped back a little behind the vertical, which leaves her swinging on his mouth, and her lower leg has come too far forward, something which goes hand in hand with the other ailments. I think the rider's expression says it all.

A somewhat better halt. The horse has good flexion in his jaw, although he's now evading by going over the bit and becoming overbent. The rider has a nice soft contact and, in accordance with all the old text books, has the classic straight line from the elbow, through the forearm and wrist, via the rein to the mouth. Again her leg position is very sound, although the foot is insecure in the stirrup. The horse isn't standing square behind, and is too far over his forelegs, which leaves him a little hunched over his feet. Note that it's always easier to school a horse in the early stages with a wall or fence as a guide. At least he'll tend to do things in straight lines.

Having finished work, the horse has halted squarely. He's relaxed in his jaw, and has an attentive expression. He's being slipped the reins as a final reward.

This is a squarer halt. The rider has a good leg position, the stirrup's hanging vertically, the rein's loose and the hand soft. The horse's hocks are slightly too far behind him but he's well over his forelegs.

There is no greater feeling than when a horse really has his hocks underneath him and is accepting the bit; when every check that the rider asks for receives an instant reaction, and when every slight opening of the hand to release a little power, and allow the horse to go forward, meets an instant upward and forward movement from the horse. Starting and stopping must be instantaneous and without question. When you put your legs on a horse and ask him to go forward he must go forward *now*, not later. It never ceases to amaze me how so many people tolerate horses being totally numb to the heel. I just do not know how they ride them.

With a horse who is totally unresponsive to the leg it is essential that he has it pointed out to him in no uncertain terms. It is a problem which can be cured in a matter of five minutes. Walk the horse about the paddock, with your stick at the ready. Give the horse a squeeze or a small kick and ask for a transition from walk to trot. If you get no reaction, give him a couple of smacks round the backside, as if you mean it. Almost every horse will shoot forward to a greater or lesser extent. It is important that you do this with an open hand on the reins, because to hit a horse with one hand and stop him going forward with the other is a contradiction and you cannot blame the horse for thinking, 'Well, just what *do* you want?' Then simply repeat the whole exercise. Give him a pat, bring him back to walk, and ask him to go forward from the legs again. If the reaction still is not instantaneous, give him another couple of smacks. It is for his own good and yours. Do not fall out with him; you are not beating him up, just furthering his education. Then give him another pat and do it all over again. I find it very rare for a horse not to improve dramatically after two or three such reminders.

It is the same when stopping a horse. If you have just jumped a big long combination, are on your way to a tall set of planks and want to shorten, it is not enough for the horse to shorten two strides after you ask him. He must respect the hand and come back to you instantly. So, as with the leg exercise, a remedy is called for. From trot or canter ask the horse to stop. If he disregards the hand and continues to run on his forehand, pull him up with some force, either with a two-handed pull, or by setting one hand on his neck and pulling with the other. Really let him know that you mean business but, again, take care not to fall out with him if you can help it.

Opposite, top: Here the horse is evading the bit by raising his head and opening his mouth.

Opposite, bottom: This shows the strength with which the horse is arguing. The rider has weakened her position by allowing the lower leg to go forward so that the seat is shallow, with no downward force. The horse has taken charge.

Lengthening and shortening

I really like the above photograph: there's such an air of 'let's go' about it. Good flat work is based on a horse going where you point him, with the power coming from behind, from the heel into the hand, which in turn controls the pace. Having worked the horse into a good shape and a short, round outline, Clare now decides to extend for a few strides down the long side of the school. It's the same as asking a horse to go forward from three or four strides out to take a fence – in both cases the response must be unquestioning and instant. Here Clare has just pulled the trigger and the horse is really powering away from her leg into a soft but guiding hand. The hands are relaxed and easy on the mouth and the horse is responding by going into the hand in an agreeable fashion. Just looking at the photograph it's almost possible to sense what a lovely feel Clare must have from the mouth: the horse is taking the bit in a light, forward-going way and she's showing him the way to the ground. The extension with the foreleg is really good and he's going well behind, with plenty of flexion of the hocks and length of stride, and with his hind legs well under him. Note the rider's excellent leg position – it's not difficult to see where the power is coming from – while at the other end the hand is most sympathetic. Horses must go both up and down gears smoothly, and this near-perfect upward transition would no doubt be followed by a downward movement into collected trot, walk or halt. Horses must at all times have their minds on what you want them to do and how they should do it. Regular changes of pace and direction are a great help in achieving that.

Taking the bend around the body. Here the rider is exaggerating the movement, but the principle is sound. It's senseless to take the rein in front of the rider and across the wither, as this merely becomes neck reining and the bend will be from the poll to the wither instead of from the poll to the tail. Moving the hand towards the hip and using the inside leg produces a bend around the rider's leg, so that the horse becomes supple all through.

There's a lot to like about this photograph; there are also one or two points to criticise about the rider. In mitigation, the camera can sometimes lie, but it does appear that I'm a little inclined here to be asking for an inside bend by taking the hand across my body instead of round it, and therefore getting more of the bend from the withers forward and not enough from behind the saddle. I also seem to be standing almost vertically in the stirrups, although the leg position is, I suppose, good enough. Who knows, perhaps a few frames later it may have been better of me and worse of the horse, who in this photograph is doing everything asked of her. Her shape is superb, she's going exactly where I point her, is making full use of the corner and is really bending around my inside leg as if it were a gatepost. Her short outline and the pressure being put on the muscles in her neck can do nothing but good for the top line.

Above: Here there's plenty of length to the horse's stride, and the rider has good rein contact. She's raising the inside hand a little to lift the head slightly. Basically, a show jumper is asked to carry his head behind the vertical so as to stretch and work all the muscles along the back and top line, but care must be taken not to allow the horse to carry his head on the forehand. He should take the rein in a genuine way, as this horse is doing. To ride a horse in this shape the rider must have the engine going. The two ends must come together so that the middle comes up and the head wants to go down.

Opposite, top: The horse in short, collected trot. After shortening exercises it's important that the horse also has a chance to extend himself.

Opposite, bottom: The horse being ridden out of the corner to extend down the long side of the school. Since this horse customarily becomes introverted in his work, he needs to lengthen his neck for a while and be 'shaken loose' before being picked up again at the end of the long side.

LIBRARY
BISHOP BURTON COLLEGE
BEVERLEY HU17 8QG

Leg yielding
It's of great benefit to a horse to perform sideways movements away from the bend, so that he learns obedience and becomes physically active and elastic. In the left-hand photograph the horse is evading in most ways: there's no recognisable bend, he's resisting the rider's leg and his overall outline is poor. In the right-hand photograph, while he isn't yet firmly established in the movement he is gradually improving. The bend is starting to form from head to tail, although he doesn't appear to be crossing his hind legs.

In many ways this is quite a powerful picture of a very powerful horse. One only has to look at the strength this fellow has behind the saddle and the strong-minded look on his face to realise that he's anything but a mug's companion. To be perfectly honest I can't remember what work Clare was doing at the moment this photograph was taken, but judging from the angle of her leg and the fact that she has her hands set on his withers, it appears that she's squeezing him upwards and forwards which, in turn, will be putting the hocks further and further underneath. This obviously works to maximum effect with the weight out of the saddle to free the hindquarters and allow the back really to come up. By restricting the front end and controlling the pace quite firmly, the end product in skilful hands can only be a shorter outline, a better shape and the creation of extra power, which in this case is obviously considerable. If a horse had ability enough, which this one certainly had, he'd jump a very big and wide fence from this sort of approach.

The Half-Halt

A half-halt on the flat is exactly the same in essence as a check on the way to a fence. If you cannot lengthen and shorten a horse at walk and trot, you will not be able to do so at canter, and the job is made even harder when someone puts a course of fences in front of you. It is, therefore, of the utmost importance for the rider to be able to make the horse go up or down a gear at will. Having established a comfortable seat in the saddle, the rider must strive to improve his horse and the ride he gives, whether for competition purposes or just to make him an agreeable mount. An ill-mannered, unschooled, disobedient hooligan of a horse can never be a pleasure to ride.

The importance of the half-halt or check cannot be over-emphasised. The horse must react promptly – on short distances between fences there is no time for argument, so the horse must believe in his rider completely. The half-halt may perhaps be defined as a retarding of the forward movement. When used it should not actually cause a horse to change from canter to trot, but should merely abbreviate the one pace. The half-halt should be followed by a forward-riding aid which, if all goes well, will create a rounder action and set up the horse with his hocks well underneath him.

The early lessons are best taught at walk, perhaps actually making the horse halt for a second or so before moving on. Also, to begin with the rider may find it more effective to have no stirrups and to take the legs away from the saddle at the exact time that the rein aid is given, causing the seat bones to come in closer contact with the saddle, and the firm, straight back to create downwards pressure. It must be stressed that if a horse resists the hand, then the rider must give to the horse and try again. A half-halt is not created by one long haul but more by a feather-light closing of the hand, to which the obedient horse will respond immediately. This will only be achieved through patience and perseverance. If you are riding in a field or school, set yourself a point where you will take a half-halt check, and ride forward immediately afterwards, even if the horse does not appear to notice. Time alone will achieve results in this exercise. If the horse does not react, take another half-halt a stride further on. This enables the rider to balance the horse and should always be used to signal a movement as a means of preparation. With time, a horse will respond to a light touch on the rein and slight pressure with the seat, and the rider will then be in a better position to execute the movement or exercise.

The half-halt

If a horse ignores the aids for half-halt or halt, there's a positive way of putting the message across without being rough. Taking a good, short contact, place your inside hand firmly on his neck as shown in the photographs. Ask for the half-halt or halt with the outside hand, bracing yourself against the inside one. Do this in a strong, positive way a couple of times. It won't harm your horse but it will improve his halt, provided you use a pull, not a snatch or jag. Once the horse takes notice, he can be ridden normally again, but don't be afraid to repeat the exercise if he becomes too strong again.

The Rein-Back

Before the rein-back is introduced into his education, the horse must be going forward freely and without hesitation. In theory, the horse should be pushed back, *never pulled*.

First, establish a good halt, keeping the rein contact but not pulling back, and then ask the horse to move gently forward into a closed hand. If he does not go back straight away, rather than cause stress move forward and try the exercise again, with increased firmness, until he moves back one stride. As soon as he moves back, ask him to go forward again, thus deriving the maximum benefit from the exercise by getting the horse's quarters underneath him and more power into the step of his hind legs.

If the horse will not rein back, it will help to have a friend stand in front of him and gently tap his coronets with a schooling whip as you apply the aids. Alternatively, try riding up to the school wall or a hedge, and then applying the correct aids. This should give the horse no option but to move backwards.

In the early stages do not ask the horse to rein back too fast or too much. Give him time to think and understand, and make sure that when he does move back he remains straight. If he goes off a straight line, adjust your leg position to behind the girth on the offending side. Use the rein-back to help with forward transitions, for example, rein-back to canter. Always keep the aids soft and never resort to harsh pulling.

Many riders, particuarly on the Continent, are seen to ask a horse to rein back during the time between entering the ring and starting a round. This is sometimes not a bad idea if a horse is becoming a little over-ambitious and running on too freely. It serves to shorten the horse up and put him into an even better shape. At the very least, it is a big help in getting the horse to think on the rider's terms or, to put it another way, to point out to the horse that the rider really is in charge. At this stage it is important above all to ask the horse to rein back in an agreeable fashion. The last thing you want just before the bell goes is to have a stand-up row with your horse.

Draw Reins

It was the great Hungarian trainer Bert de Nemethy, who until quite recently took the United States team to so many successes, who said that draw reins are like a razor in a monkey's hand. How right he was. While I do not wish to advocate their use, it has to be said that draw reins can sometimes be an extremely useful gadget when schooling

an older horse who is set in bad habits; a younger one who needs to be gently advised about where he should carry his head; or even, in some cases, with a high-spirited horse who already goes in a good shape but who may sometimes get a little above himself and need to be contained for the first few minutes of a work session.

Ideally the rider should still be working on the bit rein, merely using the draw reins as and when needed. On a horse who is giving in his jaw, the draw reins should have slight loops in them; at this stage it may be best to take them off altogether, in case the horse and rider unanimously decide to rely on them. Whilst the horse's shape may look good, it may actually be a false outline and would be better achieved without continued use of the draw reins.

On horses whom I feel derive benefit from draw reins, a useful trick is to knot the draw rein and drop it on the horse's neck, which leaves the rider to work on the horse's mouth with no more than hands and heels. Then, if the horse starts to become over-bold, and the head comes up, you merely have to put one finger around the draw reins (which sit in about the same position as a martingale

Being an older horse, and one set in his not too genteel ways, Corunna Bay, otherwise known as Tom, had to be schooled in draw reins. He was a difficult horse to hold together, hence the thick snaffle and draw reins. Other horses may need the 'advice' which draw reins give and then ideally only loose ones, which come into use only if the horse persists in carrying his head too high. Always have the main contact on the proper rein, so that the horse becomes used to the feel of that rein in conjunction with the leg, and so is less likely to raise his head as soon as the draw reins are taken off.

neckstrap) and, having re-aligned the horse's head carriage, revert to the ordinary reins again as soon as possible.

There really is no substitute for hands and heels used correctly. Although draw reins can be useful, it must be remembered that when you go into the ring you cannot take them with you – you are on your own. What you are trying to achieve *in* the ring is, wherever possible, best achieved outside it without the help of gadgets. Accessories such as draw reins can be, and are, a short-term means to an end, not an end in themselves. Care and common sense are necessary at all times, and you must always bear in mind the end product, what you are trying to achieve, and the horse's mental attitude.

CHAPTER 4

Facilities at Home

Different riders' training facilities vary enormously – from the top American rider who once told me that he possessed only six poles, to other leading establishments which have a complete facsimile of every type of fence imaginable, and certainly every obstacle likely to be encountered at such showgrounds as Hickstead and Aachen.

A horse will not know the difference between a set of fences made of oil drums and packing cases, etc, and a full-blown set bought with no expense spared. But from a convenience point of view it is certainly a great help to have fences which are easy to move and alter; poles which are neither so light that they fall down at the first puff of wind nor so heavy that they are likely to turn a horse over; and wings which hold poles upright, exactly where you want them to sit, and give a horse the focal point of a fence at which to aim.

In general, the nearer you can come to a show set of fences for training purposes, the better – and never be mean with the paint brush. Horses may or may not be colour blind: who knows? I certainly do not. But it is a fact that they react noticeably to brightly painted fences. For example, Flying Wild once crashed a back rail of a big all-red treble at the Royal Show. She never forgot it, and ever afterwards tended to make doubly sure that she was right in her approach to any red combination. Also, for several seasons in her early years, Sunorra had a thing about pushing the front rail off a rustic parallel– so for that matter, do a lot of other horses.

Some single fences need to be really bold in order to test a horse's courage in taking them on. At the other extreme, I always use a narrow stile, with poles little more than 6ft long, to teach a horse to take care about jumping that top rail. Incidentally, there never seems to be a shortage of stile poles: the odd breakage of full-length poles is inevitable and the pieces usually saw nicely to length for the stile.

It is obviously better to have too many fences, rather than too few. With a yard full of horses of varying grades, I find that having enough material on hand to build two

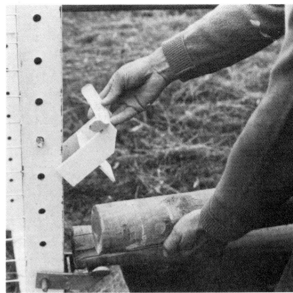

Jump cups

I've recently abandoned the old peg and chain jump fittings in favour of the ones shown in the photographs. The bar used in this model is much easier to handle than the peg and chain. When using the latter you really need three hands to alter a fence and tend to end up with a pole resting on your shoulder or under your arm, or having to bend down to put one end on the ground. The bar fittings are a lot easier and faster to use and should, I think, last longer, since there's no pin and chain to become lost. Bar fittings aren't really a new idea, but for some reason they've been slow to catch on.

Everyone has different ideas as to how deep the cups should be: as the photographs suggest, I opt for middle of the road. The cups shown are quite deep, which helps reduce the number of fallen poles that have to be picked up. However, I'm going over to lighter 10ft poles, which are better for use indoors and are much easier to handle. Even when used with a deepish cup, they'll still come down easily enough if they're hit hard. As I have a lot of students and horses to work, there is a great deal of fence alteration and pole picking up in a day, and the more the whole operation can be streamlined, the less wear and tear there is on everyone. The poles in the picture came from a local fencing company and cost only £4.00 to £5.00 each. They're machined to the same thickness and length which makes every fence look better. I love to see straight lines and to have a fence looking as it would in a competition.

I really like the metal wings pictured here. The uprights are made from box section, with holes 3in apart. The square wire mesh makes a good solid barrier when painted white and is light and durable. I have them made up locally for about the same price as a pair of wooden wings. To my mind that's good value, since they'll wear for a very long time – I've been using them for three years and haven't had a broken or bent one yet. Another advantage is the noise that the whole outfit makes when a horse touches the fence: it produces a fair old clatter, which tends to make the horse more careful next time.

courses of seven or eight fences saves a lot of hard work in altering fences to suit particular horses. Some fences can be left quite small, while others can be put at medium height, with fillers and boards, walls, and so on, under them, which are quite probably a little beyond the novice horse. I like to have at least one of each type of fence which a horse is likely to meet in competition. For everyday use, apart from a great amount of poles painted in different colours, I find that I cannot do without two separate sets of planks (I sometimes use one set with a pole behind as a parallel); a gate (preferably two, of different sizes); two walls (one small, one larger), and as many varied fillers as possible. These certainly need not be expensive; anyone with a few tools and a little handyman's flare (something which I certainly do not possess) can make up any number of additions to fences quite cheaply.

Ordinary parallel bars can be a bit repetitive and I like to vary the theme a little by using a gate or planks as the front element. As a general rule I prefer to keep my parallels square and flat across the top, as in this photograph. Always hang the gate on flat plank fittings as shown here. A gate is a weighty obstacle; the one in the photograph is made of oak and has been around for years. It needs to be in flat cups because it is nearly two peoples' work to lift it and in deep cups it could turn a horse over. For that reason alone I wouldn't jump a really green horse over it, and anyway it's a bit too big for that.

In the background are two examples of other fences which, as I said earlier, I like to have around at all times. The one on the right is a pole over a biggish solid wall standing about 4ft 3in to 4ft 6in; the smaller one on the left is typical of the easy-to-jump novice type of fence. To the left of the picture (just under the mare's hind legs) is a pile of plastic blocks specially designed for building fences. They're very useful as fillers, for propping up odd poles and especially for building the sort of lungeing fences illustrated in Chapter 1.

A bold triple bar which is ideal for getting the more experienced horse up in the air. There's a lot of material involved here and I wouldn't build too many fences like this because it ties up too much equipment. Nevertheless, it's a good fence over which to train Graded horses since it's typical of the type of fence that you'll meet regularly at the better type of show. From the training point of view this is a good fence at which to practise getting right up to the front rail. You wouldn't want to stand off it, and from a rider's point of view it takes a little practice to ride deep to that front rail. It's surprising how many riders and horses have difficulty in getting in close to a triple bar. The problem is magnified if the horse has already clouted one or two back rails, because he'll then tend to back off even more and pick up further away.

Dry ditch

A dry ditch is simple to make, using three short railway sleepers firmly staked into the ground, and need only be as deep as the width of one sleeper. The bottom should be kept clear of grass and weeds, etc, so that horses really look into it. It's amazing how many problems this little hole in the ground causes. Horses tend to dry up on the last stride, thus losing height and width. I most often use a square rustic oxer over the ditch, as shown here, and keep the top rails dead square. Horses tend to take the front rail off due to crouching and becoming heavy on the forehand. A simple variation is to remove the back rail and cups and approach the fence the other way, with the ditch in front of straight-up rails, Hickstead fashion (with or without a ground rail on the take-off edge of the ditch). This is a handy little permanent fence – small enough, when used with a tiny parallel above, for training very green horses, but still adequate, with a big fence over it, for older ones. Every time I jump it on a new horse, young or old, I'm reminded how important it is to school every horse over this type of fence right from the start. Weather permitting, I use it almost every time I give a horse a jump in the field. I tend not to use the permanent fences in wet weather so as to prevent chopping up the take-offs and landings. Ideally a horse should eventually jump this type of fence without turning a hair, just as if the ditch wasn't there.

Water ditch

This little water ditch is ideal for a horse's first introduction to water. It's made of concrete and is very simple to build – though it must be dead level, otherwise the water will run out of one end. I put the water jump bush in front of it to build a horse's confidence prior to going on to jumping the bigger water, but I also experiment with all sorts of fences over, in front of and behind the ditch.

Above and left: The same ditch as that shown on page 83, with poles behind. The average Newcomers-going-into-Foxhunter-type horse should have mastered this one.

In the background (left) is another interesting filler. There's a story concerning this one. I took a few novices to a local three-day show at Balsall Common. Some had only just started jumping and nearly all had stops or various problems at the spotted boards which were used in every class. At home I had a pair of white boards, so at six o'clock the following morning Clare set to work with a pot of black paint while I and the girls took the whole team of novices up to the field for a bit of practice. I can't recall whether or not we won any classes that same day, but I do remember that nothing stopped at those spots again. It's far better to overcome a problem in the tranquility of your own paddock, and with time to spare, than to adopt the sudden-death approach in competition.

Water jump

A water jump doesn't need to be very wide – the brush can always be pulled out a few feet on the take-off side to give it extra width. This one is 12ft across the face, to accommodate a 12ft pole as shown, and about 10ft wide, which is plenty big enough for schooling purposes, and just too big for novices.

I always start a horse off over about 4ft of water (as in the photographs on the opposite page), then work up to the bigger stretch, first by pushing the brush right into the water, but with no water showing on the take-off side. I always place a pole over the water; horses concentrate more on the pole than the water, and it gets them into the air. I'm a great believer in horses getting plenty of height at a water instead of diving for the tape.

The water shown is concrete based and is ideal; it doesn't lose water, except by evaporation, and I've laid a pipe from the main supply to it, with a tap. Every spring I paint the base with blue swimming pool paint. This photograph was taken in late autumn, which is why the whole outfit looks a bit untidy. So, too, does the field, which is ready for topping with the mower then shutting up for the winter. Note the piece of rubber matting (an old conveyor belt) on the landing edge. I don't use a lath when there is a pole over the water, but do use one

when there's no pole, as in show conditions. The simple rails alongside help to keep a young horse straight. I used to have a proper brush fence in front, but it was chewed to bits by every horse who was turned out in the field, so now I have a sloping board set on to a simple frame and painted green. It does the job just as well, is light to move around – and eliminates one more headache. The old white wings used here are the same as the standard BSJA wooden ones. They serve perfectly well but, being softwood, tend to rot and break quickly, and get chewed all too often. I'm now moving over entirely to the metal wings shown in the photographs on the preceding pages.

Care must be taken when siting a permanent water. A good length of approach from either direction is essential. Obviously, the ground needs to be flat, and the water should be situated where it can be worked into any number of sequences of fences. For example, I sometimes have it as the middle one of three, all on related distances, either in a straight line or with the fence to follow the water set at an angle. A course builder will ask questions like that, so why not practise at home? It's an excellent exercise for lengthening and shortening, and encourages a horse literally to take water in his stride.

CHAPTER 5

Early Jumping

The time spent giving the horse a sound basic education on the flat is largely a means to an end, that end being the jump itself. The quality of the actual jump a horse makes is governed by two factors: firstly, a sound approach, which is dependent upon the horse's confidence and the degree of accuracy and control achieved by the rider; secondly, the horse's ability. If a horse has little or no natural jumping ability, no amount of groundwork and schooling will alter that fact; but if he has a natural jump, then a good, sympathetic, intelligent education will make the young horse's job so much easier that it will be possible to improve and make the best use of his capabilities. Furthermore, making life easier for a horse gives him more incentive. He should then be able to develop his ability to the full and, thanks to a sound mental approach, to make use of it over a long period of time. A horse needs to be relaxed and happy in his work if he is to retain his enthusiasm for jumping fences, which is really an unnatural occupation for him. One does not see many horses winning big competitions when they are under extreme pressure and obviously not enjoying their work.

So where do you start? With a horse who is just broken and is riding reasonably well on the flat, or one who has had a bad initial education over fences, the first thing is to build up his confidence or to revive his enthusiasm. This can only be achieved by minimising the risk of hurting or frightening him and by ensuring that at all times he is performing with a good heart and a steady frame of mind.

The pole on the ground is of course the first stage for every horse. Approaching at walk, let the horse come backwards and forwards and from either rein a few times until there is a total absence of 'spook' about his approach. From there, progress to two poles about 5ft apart. Now move on to a nice swinging working trot, keeping a definite yet delicate contact with the horse's mouth whilst softly pushing him up into the bridle with the lower leg. Always

remember that the horse is a rear-engined animal and that the power comes from the back to the front – or, if you like, from the heel into the hand. Bear in mind the old riding school maxim, 'Put your horse in balance and ride him forward.'

It is a golden rule of show jumping that a horse must always be allowed plenty of time to think about what he is doing. There is a fine dividing line between putting enough pressure on him to keep him up to his work, and overdoing the pressure and pace so that his brain becomes scrambled and he makes mistakes. When that happens you are doing more harm than good.

I always like to introduce my novices to their proper jump with a couple of poles crossed at the centre of the fence. This gives the horse a point to aim for (the lowest) and, more important, keeps him where he should always be: in the centre of the fence. Novices learn bad habits all too easily, and running down a fence to one side or the other is one of them. This can soon be followed by running out altogether or hitting the wing.

The crossed poles are best sited about 9ft from the place pole and need not be any higher than 12 to 18in. When the horse is negotiating this small obstacle successfully from both reins there are many options open to the rider. Commonsense must now prevail. While it is encouraging to have a young horse making rapid progress, you should

My favourite introduction fence for a real novice or, for that matter, an older horse being prepared and limbered up for a work session over fences. The crossed poles look after the direction, the pole on the ground at its base gives the take-off point clear definition and the place pole in front of it looks after the stride and takes away the responsibility from the rider. When approached at trot the place pole is best set about 9ft from the fence. When jumping a green horse it's best to use poles like these that are at least 12ft long, and decent wings to add a bit of width. If a horse came to this fence several times, I would want him to turn left at the rails one time, right the next and so on, to prevent his anticipating the corner. It's important when landing over a fence that the horse looks to the rider for guidance where direction and pace are concerned. He must take that bend after the fence and before the paddock railings on the rider's terms; he shouldn't fall round the corner and take any old line.

An uncomplicated fence which a green horse finds easy to negotiate from canter. Again, the crossed poles keep him in the middle and going in the right direction. The ground line gives him a clearly defined take-off point, and the back rail adds a bit of height and width. This, incidentally, is a fence which I frequently use to test a young horse's ability and to find out in the early stages whether he can get sufficient height. It wouldn't be unreasonable to ask a useful young horse to jump this fence with both the crossed poles and the back rail raised gradually to about 4ft or even a little more. You certainly wouldn't have to jump any higher to gain a reliable indication of how good your horse might one day be. That apart, this really is an excellent fence for building up a young horse's confidence. It would be difficult to hit it hard unless it were jumped without enough impulsion to make the spread. Consequently the horse is unlikely to give himself a fright by clouting a pole hard early in his career.

bring each training session to an end while things are going well. Remember, there is always tomorrow.

When beginning a training session it is wise to run briefly through the previous day's work while the horse is still fresh, to check that he has mastered everything so far. When the horse has mastered the first jump from trot, a small vertical fence placed about 20ft from the crossed poles will lead him into his first jump from canter. The distance between fences at this stage obviously depends a lot on the size of the horse or pony and the length of his stride, how strongly he is taking on the fence, and his general attitude to things. Another important advantage of the crossed pole introduction to fences is that it helps the rider to place the horse correctly at the next fence. If he can keep the horse balanced and going into the bridle, there is no need for the rider to alter the horse's stride or to make any change of pace. Any serious interference from the rider at this stage will only tend to take the horse's mind off the fence. Again, a light but definite feel on the reins and a firm, variable pressure from the legs keeps the horse thinking forward, an attitude that is essential to him throughout his working life.

At this point in the horse's training you can either change to several different fences – all still worked up to as previously – or add another fence or two to the existing combination. I am a great believer in teaching novices to

jump down lines of fences well. In competition the majority of mistakes come at the double or treble, so it pays to educate the youngster to negotiate combinations properly from the earliest stages. Later in a horse's career he will often be asked to jump a wide parallel coming out of a combination, and to do this correctly he will have to have jumped in well, with care and confidence. Train him to do so when he needs your help and while the fences are still very low.

Trotting to Fences – Placing Poles

There is a lot to be achieved by working young horses over fences from trot. Because the pace is so much slower than canter, there is less chance of things going wrong. It is easier to control the pace and to govern the direction, and the youngster has more chance to think about what he is doing and to concentrate on jumping a particular fence.

It goes without saying that the rider's position and seat must be sound. He must not get left behind, at the same time giving the horse a snatch in the mouth. He should ride the horse forward, in balance, from a level pace, and should be able to go up or down a gear at his discretion.

In the early stages a fence such as the one pictured on page 87 should be used, but with more experience quite useful sized fences (all vertical) may be employed. A horse usually gets his shoulders well up and his hocks underneath

A more complicated exercise. Here the non-jumping stride has been more clearly defined by the use of place poles before and after the first part of a small vertical double. This particular combination would be a little too complicated for a really green horse but would be a good exercise for a horse with a little more mileage, in particular one who tends to rush fences and makes up too much distance in combinations. Rather than rushing headlong at the second vertical, the horse will tend to concentrate on the second pole on the ground. This will enable him to get his priorities right and literally to take one step at a time. To make a double bounce fence, add another pair of wings and poles to the second place pole – this will keep the horse's shoulders in the air and stop him running on his forehand after the first part. Many variations can be created with fences and poles on the ground but the rider must have a clearly defined picture in his mind of just what he's trying to achieve.

him when trotting deep to a fence and, when there is no interference from the rider, will bascule and round himself naturally.

More fences can now be added. The place pole and crossed poles can be followed by any amount of fences in one line. Young horses must be taught to face lines of fences fearlessly, without shrinking away from them or rushing blindly to the other side in order to get the job over and done with as quickly as possible.

Grid Work

As long as it is carefully thought out, and accurate distances are used, grid work can be of great benefit to the training programme – not only in teaching horses to jump combinations of fences. In grids at home I always keep the distances a little on the short side, in the vast majority of cases shorter than a horse would meet in a competition. I can see little point in spending hours schooling a horse on the flat to go in a short, round outline, only to open him up by asking him to jump long distances in grids, doubles or trebles. Horses learn to jump flat easily enough when the pressure is on in competition.

The following is an example of a simple grid which is a favourite of mine: a place pole, 9ft to crossed poles, 18 to 20ft (according to the length of the horse's stride) to a small vertical and then about 23ft to a parallel. This in turn could be followed, a short distance later, by another

A useful filler to start off with. This fence is simply a pair of rustic boards made from sawn-down rustic poles nailed to a framework. It's solid but not spooky and I find it ideal for introducing a horse to fillers. The look of concentration on this horse's face tells it all. The rider is sitting in a superb position; she's going forward with the movement of the horse, with plenty of support from the leg, straight to the middle of the fence; her weight is forward and her hands soft. In this position, there's no way that she's going to be left behind should the horse tend to back off.

parallel. The distance between the two parallels can subsequently be shortened within reason by bringing the two inside rails together a little, thus making the horse round himself over the two oxers and at the same time containing him on that shorter distance.

An alternative would be to do without the second parallel but to have a vertical or parallel or a set of planks off a related canter distance perhaps three or four strides away.

Bounce Fences

Some riders and trainers make use of bounce fences in training – that is a combination of fences with no non-jumping stride between them. This is all down to personal preference and although a bounce fence is excellent for shortening a horse up and getting him to be quick in front, I personally prefer to do that from the saddle and by using short distances with one non-jumping stride.

Fillers

When trotting a novice to fences I find it beneficial to add a few small fillers – low walls and strange objects such as oil drums, straw bales, etc – as soon as a horse is negotiating poles confidently. A horse must learn to take any fence in his stride without spooking and thinking backwards. Again, keep each fence small and come from trot, so that the approach can be more accurate and controlled.

If the horse is trotting to the boards confidently, the next logical step is to come from canter. Here the rider has given this young horse every chance to make a good jump and the mare's doing her bit to perfection. The shape's really good: she's going forward with confidence. Following one or two jumps like this the next step should be to add a pole over the boards and then possibly two more wings and a pole to make a spread. The rider, Tina Youngman, is sitting in a near perfect position. Perhaps to be hypercritical the hands could be a little further forward, but there's no tension in the hand and the contact, light as it is, adds support and is complemented by the support from the perfectly positioned lower leg. Tina originally came to me as a 17-year-old for one year and finished up staying for three. She's a very talented rider and was a great asset to the yard, being as much at home schooling young horses as she is now competing at international level. A dedicated rider, who understands the mechanics of the horse, she has the patience to spend any amount of time educating horses.

The importance of good hands cannot be over-emphasised. The word good really means sympathetic and caring. The hands are there to guide and advise the horse in direction and pace and should never be abused.

The two pictures are a good example of a rider making intelligent use of her hands in a relatively difficult situation. It's obvious from the first picture that this mare, having learned her early lessons well, has now, like most horses at that stage of their education, fallen into the trap of becoming over-confident and too bold in her approach to fences. She's running against the hand and bounding along with far too much impulsion for her own good. The off-foreleg and taut muscles everywhere tell you that. Just from Tina's face alone you can see what she's thinking: steady, wait a second. She's trying to slow down the movement and abbreviate the stride without getting the horse's head too high in the air and taking her concentration off the fence. Again, she's sitting in a perfect position and trying to hold the horse off the fence.

One gets the impression from this photograph that the mare would run straight into the fence if left to her own devices. If she gave herself a nasty crack in front, it might draw her attention to the fact that fences are to be respected, but it might also give her a fright, which she hardly needs at this stage of her education. The fence, incidentally, is the second half of a 24ft double, and this exercise is one that I find useful with horses of all ages. The very short approach makes sure that the rider gets the horse around the inside leg. The pace and radius of the circle are governed by the first half of the double and an over-bold horse like this one doesn't get the benefit of a long run to the fence. With a long approach on an over-ambitious horse there's always the tendency for the fence to draw the horse to it and consequently for him to be going a lot too sharply when he gets there, merely from over-concentration. There's a lot to be said for a rider waiting for the fence to come to him. Give the horse time to think.

A split second later and here the situation has changed completely, with Tina obviously calling the mare's bluff. She's saying, 'Okay, I've done everything I can for you in the approach, now you're on your own.' Without the support of the hand, the mare has suddenly found herself in a bit of a heap at the base of the fence, running on her forehand with only herself to blame. The angle of her body and hind legs suggests that she's having to back off in a hurry, and her concentration has suddenly switched from running against Tina's hand to that top rail, which is now coming at her mighty quickly. I've no doubt that she'll jump it, but after two or three approaches like this, and one or two reassuring pats, the penny will, one would hope, drop and she may well see the sense in coming from a more level approach.

CHAPTER 6

More Advanced Work

It is pointless going on to bigger and better things until a horse can canter to fences in balance, going where the rider points him at an even pace and totally under the rider's control. He must be able to lengthen and shorten to a single fence and listen to the rider before attempting anything more complicated. I find that there is a fine dividing line when it comes to how much work to do at one single fence. On the one hand it is a good thing for the horse to be casual and relaxed in his approaches because that way it is easier to get him on the rider's wavelength, but on the other hand horses can soon become bored and complacent about continually jumping the same fence and it is better at that point to move on to another one, or to reverse the fence and come the other way, just to give the horse a fresh feel about it.

The preparation for a fence is best done sooner rather than later. It is hopeless to allow a horse to cart you all the way to a fence and then have to compensate for a bad approach in the last two strides, either by snatching him up to stop him running into the fence, or kicking and slapping him to make sure of getting over. Make your arrangements plenty far enough away. Make the most of what space you have available, especially in an indoor school. You simply cannot afford to give space away indoors and leave one or two strides in the corner. Set the horse up from a long way out, keep him between hand and heel and always try to have him waiting for your instructions. Let the fence come to you but at the same time support the horse both mentally and physically with the leg.

Seeing a Stride
There is no doubt in my mind that from a trainer's point of view teaching a rider to judge a stride into a fence is far and away the most difficult task of all. Basically it is down to natural ability: education and training count for very little compared to a reasonably accurate natural eye. But, as I have said before, I also firmly believe that a jump is basically the result of the direct preparation which

precedes it. It follows that the more controlled and professional the approach to the fence, the easier it is to adjust the horse's stride, and therefore the all-important lengthening or shortening of the stride becomes much easier.

In fairness to riders, I should add that some horses are far easier to ride to fences than others. To quote an example of a horse which everyone knows, Ryan's Son must have been a dream to ride to a fence because he would literally have given you a choice of six strides on the way to every one. He had a short, skipping action and could lengthen and shorten as well as any horse that I have ever seen. Such a horse gives a rider many options on the way to a fence and any one of them could be the right one. The opposite would be the headstrong horse who does not shorten easily and is perhaps over-bold as well. On a horse like that you really have to pick up a stride as you go along and go on the one that is given to you.

Seeing a stride is almost totally dependent on confidence. If the rider has a hang-up about it – and so many do – the problem simply gets worse instead of better and usually shows up in two distinct ways. The commonest fault is for the rider to fiddle indecisively with the horse's mouth all the way to the fence instead of making one major adjustment and then coming again. If you cannot see the makings of a stride four or five strides out, you really have to do something about it; keeping the leg on to keep the horse coming forward and going into the fence, you have to take a firm check to alter the horse's stride, and make some adjustment to the distance between you and the fence.

Riding a course of fences is all about adding and substracting. You either have to come more strongly to a fence and lengthen a stride, or hold the horse up together and shorten the last few strides, in order to meet that particular fence at the right point of take-off. But I think that there are a couple of golden rules which should be obeyed. Firstly, you must have about three strides going forward. Secondly, the last stride must always be the strongest.

It follows that excessive fiddling in front of a fence can only result in a horse reaching the fence with no impulsion, probably still on a bad stride and, worst of all, unbalanced and with his head in the air because of the aggravation he has suffered from the saddle in the previous six strides.

The other option is the one where the rider, in trying to avoid the situation just described, kicks for the long stride, sometimes from a long way out, on the assumption that pace alone will make up for inaccuracy. It does not work that way, and you can certainly run into far more trouble from that sort of approach. However, I prefer the novice rider who does something decisively, and does it wrongly, than the one who sits and does nothing, and still does it wrongly.

Practice makes perfect and there is no doubt that the more fences you jump the more accurate you generally become. Training and education are one thing – everyone needs guidance on technique – but this particular problem is so much down to rider ability that to a great extent he is on his own. Having been pointed in the right direction, he really needs to go away and work at it. Obviously, you cannot wear out one horse simply to keep practising your strides. If you have access to more than one, it is an advantage; but however many horses you ride, if you are jumping for your own benefit, not theirs, keep the fences very small – and I mean *very* small. There is no point in wearing out a horse by jumping decent sized fences merely to practise seeing a stride. It is the approach you are working on, not the fence.

What is more, the bigger the fence, the more it will influence the horse's approach. A biggish fence will encourage a bold, generous horse to think, 'This is a little on the big side; we really ought to be going somewhere, instead of all the messing about that he is doing in the saddle.' Or, conversely, 'That looks a bit big; let's make sure we get it right or I don't want to know.' Either way it is not going to help the rider to maintain a level approach. On the other hand, if the fence is really small, the horse will approach it in a more relaxed manner, will have no reason for any violent change of pace or attitude, and will therefore give his rider a better chance to be more accurate. Nothing succeeds like success; if a rider really feels that he has cracked it over small fences, he will become more confident, and from then on his approaches and strides should become better.

The value of a sound approach cannot be over-emphasised, because if the horse is collected, balanced and going forward in a good shape, he can cope with being a bit too far off or a bit too close. If a rider is a full half-stride out, then that really is a problem and no horse will stand for it for very long. But it is amazing how, up to a certain level, horses learn to cope with a not unreasonable degree of inaccuracy as long as the approach is sound. Accepting that a non-jumping stride is around 12ft, then the worst you can be is 6ft too far off or too close and it really is impossible for a horse to cope with that incessantly: no one should blame a horse for packing it in at some stage of the game. But, as I have said, as long as the build-up to the fence is sound and knowledgeable, it is not asking too much of a capable horse to get used to jumping fences from 2 to 3 ft too close or too far away in novice classes. When you come to fences of 3 ft 9in to 4ft and above, a greater degree of accuracy is essential. No horse can consistently jump big courses from bad strides. The horse is basically a forgiving creature and if the rider generally does a decent job, the horse will forgive him the odd miss. On the other hand, if a rider is so inaccurate that he jumps from more bad strides than good ones, then he must restrict his riding to a level at which the horse can cope with his inaccuracy, and not attempt to jump the sort of course that will shatter the horse's confidence.

There really is no overnight cure for a bad eye for a stride. I am convinced that all a trainer can do is to work on the approach, preserve the horse's confidence and, having put the rider on the right lines, tell him to go away and practise at a level that he and the horse can cope with easily.

Where to Take Off

I am often asked what a rider should look at on the way to a fence. Should it be the top rail or the ground line or some point round about the take-off? I do not really think that there is any hard and fast rule, and to be perfectly honest I could not really say what I look at myself in the approach. I think that maybe I look at the fence as a whole, bearing in mind that there is a different technique involved for different fences.

This is a fair illustration of getting a horse in close to a fence, and this mare is making a nice round outline over an unimposing fence. She is in fact a bit loose with her near fore, which is unlike her as we'll see in the next chapter. But she's still a little novicy in her jump, only being a six-year-old, so I think she can be excused for that. Because she's in close, she's really having to work and get her shoulders up and to back off the fence. For my part, all I have to do is to go with her and follow the movement. She's rounding herself nicely and seems totally happy with the contact, and my hand would suggest that if she needed more rein she'd be quite welcome to take it.

I would always prefer a horse to take off too close to a fence rather than too far away. It is pointless spending hours training a horse to operate from a short, round stride, only to undo it all by continually standing him off fences. It is far less wearing on the animal to get in close to a fence than continually to stretch him by having him a yard off all the time. Obviously, with fences such as triple bars, staircase oxers and, above all, water jumps, you really need to get the horse in as deep as possible. But there is an awful lot to be gained, too, by having a horse close to big verticals, as long as the stride is short and you have the horse between your leg and the fence, encouraging him to snap up in front and get his shoulders in the air.

Jumping a Small Course
Having put in the necessary groundwork with the young horse, the next step is to take a well-thought-out trip round a course of small fences. I am a great believer in the value of confidence in both horse and rider, and only when the rider is sure in his own mind that his preparation has been sound and the horse is ready is it time to tackle a course. It is best not to risk giving the horse a fright by rushing him at fences which he is obviously not ready to take on.

If the schooling sessions have been going well, with each one ending on a happy note, then the whole thing can be put together with an eye to the horse's first competition. But before the youngster has his first outing in public, it is wise to have him performing fluently round a few small courses at home. It is even more important that he has jumped through a variety of doubles, so that he goes into his first competition full of confidence in himself and his rider.

It is now that the hours spent schooling on the flat, trotting to fences, grid work and cantering to small single fences should bear fruit. A satisfactory jump is the direct result of a sound approach, the approach being governed by the degree of obedience that the horse has learned from his schooling. Schooling is a means to an end. The end itself is a controlled, balanced round at the right pace, with the horse taking a line determined by the rider and arriving at each fence at a point of take-off from which he will find it easy to negotiate each obstacle.

The beauty of schooling over a course of fences at home is that it is never necessary to allow the horse to attempt a fence from a less than satisfactory approach. If the rider feels that everything is not as it should be, it is always possible to stop and start again, or circle and start afresh.

Remember, a horse usually jumps a fence in a manner largely influenced by what happened at the previous one, so it follows that if he has made a poor job of one fence, he is likely to do the same at the next. What is the point of allowing him to build up bad habits?

I rarely jump big fences at home on any grade of horse, and firmly believe it is best to school the young horse over fences a little smaller than those he will meet in the ring. This, again, builds up confidence, and gives the horse the feeling that he is well up to his job and able to take on anything his rider asks. If he believes in you, he will rarely question your judgement.

Before setting out to jump a horse over his first full course, it pays to jump him over each fence as an individual element. This can be done over a short period of time while the horse is being worked in and given his canter work. Particular attention should be given to ensuring that he is jumping fluently through the double. Keep it low and build it up a hole at a time until he is really taking you to it.

As I said in Chapter 5, I more often than not build doubles and trebles a little shorter at home than they are in competition. Since the aim is to get the horse to operate from a short, round stride, there is no point in making him reach for the second element: it only results in his jumping flat, and landing with less control than is required to get to the next fence. Before jumping a course for the first time, make sure that the horse is going nicely, in a well-balanced canter, at a level pace and with good rhythm. If this can be maintained over a series of fences without any major changes of pace, you are doing your job well.

Horses usually fall into one of two main groups – those who take their fences too strongly, and those who need driving into them. What you should look for is the happy medium. As in his flat work, the horse should be thinking 'forward' but in an agreeable fashion, not blindly rushing to get to the other side. With a horse who rushes, it is usually wise to circle a few times between fences to switch him off a little. If he persists in boiling over, come down to trot, or even walk, then pick him up again. If you feel it would help, trot him over an upright or two. In competition, I often trot a hot-headed novice round a corner or two, or even over an occasional fence if I think it will help him to settle. Remember, things happen so much more slowly from trot, and there is less chance of a wholesale blunder which would go a long way towards wrecking his confidence. Trot will give him time to think what he is doing.

Always go straight to the middle of the fence and at right angles to the poles: basically nothing less than 90° will do. Allowing a horse consistently to jump fences at angles prevents him from using his natural ability to the full. For example, in jumping a fence from left to right, the horse is obliged to lead with his off fore. Consequently he loses power from his near hind, and the end result is a slither rather than a jump. A jump from right angles to the fence invariably results in both front legs and shoulders coming up together, as a pair, and a good follow through, encouraging the horse to use his hindquarters correctly.

Don't look down over the fence – it's too late to do anything about that one. Look ahead for the next and keep in mind the line you want to take. It's obvious from the expression on the German-bred Granita's face where her attention is: where it should be, on the next fence. This is a superb illustration of how a horse should bend her legs. To be very critical, she looks a little headlong here and a bit quick through the air. She's also perhaps leaning slightly to one side. But she was a very neat jumper and although she lacked a bit of distance down combinations, she didn't have many fences down.

With the other type of horse – the one who is reluctant to take on a fence – have him going well up into the bridle from a very strong leg. If you have a fence down, it is always preferable to have it down with the front legs. This usually teaches him to be more careful. But hanging his hind legs up on the back rail of a spread will frighten him and things will tend to go from bad to worse. He will remember hurting himself, will be even more wary, and at the very next spread he may do exactly the same thing again.

The line from one fence to the next should always be in a rider's mind, particularly around corners. When turning a corner, always keep your eye on the fence you are approaching. Do not look down – the hands and legs should be quite capable of working without being observed. Likewise, do not look down while in mid-air over a fence. It is too late to do anything about that one, so look ahead to the next. With a forward-thinking attitude the rider will subconsciously encourage the horse to look for the next fence himself, making the approach simpler because both horse and rider are ready for it. Around corners, always be aware of the line you wish to take to the next fence. Do not come at an angle: always go straight to the middle of the pole, at right angles to it. Remember that horses learn bad habits easily enough without being encouraged to jump across fences at bad angles through careless approaches. If the rider gets into the habit of using his corners well at home, he will ride them better in the ring without having to think about it.

When planning to take your horse to his first competition, it is worth taking an extra amount of time to make doubly sure that he is ready before his first class. Horses get used to their own fences at home, and when taken to a show can go right back to square one. It might not be a bad plan to find a friend in your locality who has a few show jumps, and ask if you could come over for a dress rehearsal. Build a small course and work your horse in as usual. Give him a few pops over a couple of fences, then jump over the whole course. If he takes to it well and pleases you, then you are in business. If not, it is back to the drawing board – there is always tomorrow.

If your horse is going well and is doing his best to please, never hesitate to give him a pat or a few words of encouragement. He must always associate jumping with enjoyment and be happy in his work. If things are not going too well, do not pick a fight with him without first asking yourself what is going wrong. Is it your fault or his? It is always best to *think your way* through a problem rather than try to *have your way* through sheer force alone.

In competition, most mistakes are made at combination fences, so it would make sense, if you have enough fences, to practise over doubles and trebles until they become as simple to a horse as single fences. Again, in most cases it is better to practise over short distances to prevent a horse losing his shape and to keep him up in the air. Obviously, if a horse is having problems making distance out of a double, you must simply train him to cope with that distance at home. The best method would be to start short and gradually increase the length and width so that the horse is soon jumping to the full extent of his capabilities without realising it. It will at least prove to him that he can do it. But keep the fences on the small side, at least for the first few efforts.

Jumping doubles and trebles successfully is mostly down to the approach and the way a horse is trained to jump in. If he does not get in well, he has less chance of getting out. He must be going somewhere, in a good shape and at the right pace, and with plenty of power coming through from behind. It is far better to clout a pole in front going in than to hang up on a back rail coming out. With sufficient training he should avoid doing either.

Within reason it does no harm to have a fair bit of width on the spreads. Horses must learn to make the back rail, and it is no good kidding yourself at home then running into trouble the first time you meet something at maximum width in the ring.

The Flying Change

Show jumping is largely a matter of getting from A to B in as agreeable a fashion as possible, with the horse going where you point him and at the pace which you dictate. In any course of fences there are a number of changes of direction and different lines to be taken. In most cases a horse will land on the correct leg for the next bend or turn – largely because, either consciously or subconsciously, the rider has made some fundamental changes of position, has offered a little advice through hands and heels and in all probability has shifted his body weight in the anticipated direction, all of which influences the horse to land into his stride on the correct leg.

However, it is not always that simple. Some horses have little regard for direction and will land on the leg they favour come what may; others habitually take off on one leg and land on the other. To make life easier, both in competition and in everyday schooling work, time should be spent on teaching the young (or older) horse to perform

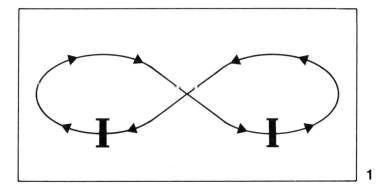

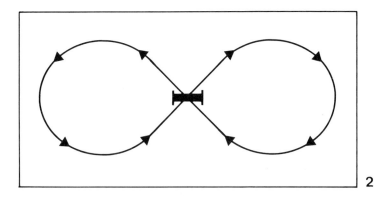

the flying change. I start by using a small fence or crossed poles as the change point. I usually site the fence in the middle of the school or against the wall, in any case quite close to the outside track, in order to take advantage of the wall or boundary fence. The fence should be at right angles to the wall. As a result, the horse's outline will have an inside lateral bend in anticipation of the following corner. Two fences can be used to teach the horse on either leg, as in figure 1. Once past this early stage a horse should soon learn to change on to either leg at the centre of a figure of eight, with or without the aid of a small fence, as shown in figure 2.

To prepare a horse for flying change, practise changing legs by a downward transition to trot for a couple of strides then strike off to canter again at once; the subsequent change of pace, both up and down, will at least give the horse an idea of what is required and will concentrate his mind on your actions. When asking for flying change, remember that the horse can only achieve it if he is light in the hand and well over his legs, with his hocks well under him. Timing is everything, and the rider must ask at the precise moment that the horse is best able to perform it.

The aids are the same as in collected canter on a small circle and for strike-off from walk to canter. The outside leg should be well back to prevent the horse's quarters from drifting outwards; aim for a good inside bend, with the inside hind leg well under, the horse soft in the mouth and with as great a degree of collection as possible. With an upward and forward movement the inside heel asks the horse to change legs and to strike off on to the opposite leg. Do not let him become wound up with this exercise since it will be twice as hard to teach him if he is worried. A little extra time and patience will pay off handsomely.

How Much Work?

Because they are all individuals, horses have widely differing needs when it comes to training, schooling, exercise and general fitness work. Whatever his particular needs, each horse's work schedule should be as varied as possible, since boredom must be avoided at all costs.

How often does one read of work programmes extending over weeks and sometimes months, in which authors have set out strict regimes for the exercise and education of horses? It simply does not work that way. Commonsense and a day-to-day appraisal of the situation is sufficient to tell a practised eye how much a particular horse needs at any given time. You can no more generalise about horses' work requirements than you can about their diets. You certainly do not feed every horse the same, so how can you expect every horse to thrive and improve on a pre-determined, long-term plan, with no commonsense feel for what a horse does or does not require at that particular time?

My horses' programme is based on as entertaining a mix as possible of work on the flat, gymnastics, work over fences, hacking, general fitness work and the all-important recreation periods spent browsing in the paddocks. As a general rule, my horses would perhaps have, assuming they were in strong work, two reasonably serious work-outs per week on the flat; one session a week going for a longish amiable hack round the country lanes (the quieter the better if that is possible in this mechanical age), and one day working on longish canter sessions to increase their stamina and blow out their wind. These sessions, which are greatly enjoyed by all, may take the form of long work around the edge of the biggest field on the place, when a lead horse jumps off in front, with the rider knowing exactly how fast he or she wants to go, and every other horse falling into line behind at intervals of ten horse lengths apart. I have one field ideally suited to this kind of

work, where it is possible to go one complete circuit and pull up on a reasonable incline. Alternatively, I give all the horses – but more often the thick-winded ones – a series of sharp breeze-ups along the headland of a field, pulling up at the top, and walking down to the bottom again to allow the horses to catch their breath, before repeating the process. The horses are allowed to jump off and really stride along for a few hundred yards at a smart pace, though always on the bridle. They love it and certainly do not regard it as work. Consequently the following day's work goes with more of a swing; the horses are fitter, brighter and more mentally alert. It makes a welcome change for the riders and grooms, too.

Incidentally, as in loose schooling, I never hack horses out on the roads without protective kneeboots.

How Much Jumping?

The amount of jumping a horse requires at home is, of course, largely governed by how much competition work you do. Most older horses need very little jumping at home. They get quite enough wear and tear on the Grade A circuit without having additional work put on them unless, of course, they have a problem which needs ironing out. However, the average novice will certainly benefit

This isn't a fence that I'd build very often, but occasionally you'll find a horse who habitually takes the front rail off a parallel. Laying a pole across the front of the fence in this way can help, as a short-term method, to get the horse up in the air and to respect the fence. But, having said that, I'd be the first to admit that it's definitely a fabrication and I'd only use this method as a last resort or when running out of ideas. If a horse isn't capable of jumping a quite bold parallel like this one without the aid of a sloping pole, then in my view he isn't good enough anyway. Even so, certain horses do benefit from a bit of help of this kind, both in their early education and, sometimes, much later in their careers.

from being given a few jumps on a fairly regular basis.

One of the best ever producers of top-class novices was the late Len Carter, who once said to me, 'I like to keep giving them a little jump.' There is more to that simple statement than meets the eye, and I am sure that Len was right because the emphasis must certainly be on little and often. Never run a horse into the ground, or send him back to his stable exhausted; always try to finish on a good note, with the horse in a contented frame of mind and quite happy to come out next time and do the same again, if not more.

In general, I also tend to jump a horse at home over a few inches less height and width than he would meet in competition, on the basis that it is less taxing, less wearing and builds confidence far more than hammering down to big, wide fences can ever do. I am certainly not averse to hanging a fence or two up a few holes when things are going well: it does no harm to get a horse up in the air every now and again. You sometimes need to prove to him (and yourself) that he can find a bit more height and width when he needs to. But, basically, play it softly and make everything a steady progression towards those days when it really counts. In that way you will have more horse left to call on.

In a general work-out over fences I invariably start, after having limbered up on the flat, by trotting to a crossed poles or small rail. After a couple of times the fence can be raised 3 to 6in, or perhaps a little more, and then, when it has reached 2ft 6in or 3ft, I strike off and come from canter. The fences can then be put a couple of holes higher, and having come again two or three more times, a horse should be ready to go and take on a small course.

Having jumped a full course, I usually give a horse a short break, possibly letting him amble around the field for a few minutes on a loose rein, or come back and do the whole thing again – perhaps at a hole or two higher – straight away while he is on the boil. Again, this depends on the individual. Perhaps the second time round I will increase the height of some fences by a hole or two and pull one or two of the spreads out. If the horse comes back and pleases me again, that is usually the time to give him a pat, a pull of grass and say okay, that will do for today.

If there were one or two areas I was not quite happy with, I would perhaps ask the horse to come back and just jump one or two odd fences again, always with a view to finishing on a good note, which is mentally beneficial to both horse and rider (and certainly trainer).

When training, I tend to work on mistakes at the time

that they happen, not minutes later. If a horse has a fence down, I will in most cases bring him back immediately to that fence and jump it again so that he associates having a fence down with being corrected for it, though in an agreeable fashion. If he has jumped four or five other fences before returning to that one fence, he will most likely have forgotten all about it. Likewise, if a horse is halfway through a sequence of fences and things are not going well, I would far rather pull up horse or student and give the situation a moment or two's thought or discussion and then start again, than aimlessly blunder along with things getting no better, and more likely becoming worse.

Loose Schooling
From time to time I spend a morning giving virtually everything in the yard a refreshing break from regulation work by having a loose schooling session. As usual the work varies from horse to horse, not so much in quantity but more in terms of how little or how much the individual is asked to jump. Again, the individual horse's characteristics need to be taken into consideration. A timid horse, who is over-cautious and would fall apart the first time he cracked a pole, needs to have everything made ultra-simple so that the chances of his giving himself a fright are minimal. His fences need to be well sloped on the take-off side, with no hint of a difficult groundline. For example, the old couple of crossed poles a foot or two in front of a vertical fence provides an ideal lead to a fence. Any combination fences for this horse must be built to a spot-on distance, not so short as to stop him dead in his tracks, nor so long as to make him struggle or tend to put in two strides where one is expected.

On the other hand, the over-bold horse can, if his temperament allows, draw great benefit from working out techniques for himself when jumping loose. For this horse, perhaps two or three fences on short, related distances down each side of the school is the best plan. In any case, in almost every training session at home, both for ridden exercises and for loose schooling, I build distances just a foot or two shorter than I would expect a horse to jump in a competition. Since training show jumpers is all about working on short, round strides, there is simply no point in spending half your life training the horse to go off that sort of stride on the flat, and then continually jumping him over flat fences and long distances, which immediately opens him up again and undoes all the good work spent teaching him to go in a short outline.

Rather like grid work, loose schooling a bunch of horses is something of a major operation, and a little forward planning makes life a lot easier. I tend to stand in the middle of the school myself where, apart from supervising the work each horse does, I am also in a better position to have fences adjusted and to observe at close quarters how a horse is performing. An assistant positioned at each end of the school will ensure that the horse does not cut off the corners or whip round and go back the opposite way. Another assistant is required in the centre to adjust the fences, which sometimes needs to be done without too much of a hold-up in the work. Sometimes, to avoid a break in continuity, a rail needs to be replaced smartly before the horse comes round again.

Without the aid of a rider the over-bold horse will certainly sometimes run into the odd fence which, from a schooling point of view, is no bad thing – they have got to learn. But for this reason I never loose school any horse without the protection of a pair of kneecaps. There is no sense in giving a horse a big knee unnecessarily. Tendon boots and overreach boots complete the leg protection. Unless a horse goes close behind and brushes, I tend to be less concerned about protecting the hind legs. In any case, I do not believe in over-protecting the horse's legs unless he is likely to injure himself by brushing, striking or overreaching.

I think the way I would set up a fence for loose schooling needs explaining. Without a rider, horses soon learn the knack of nipping out to one side or the other, and although the walls obviously form a barrier on the one side, on the other side it is certainly wise to make a simple lane with poles. In most cases just a single pole some 3 to 4ft from the ground is adequate.

Start slowly and over very small fences, as when schooling from the saddle during the early stages of training. The old familiar crossed poles set very low are an ideal introduction to the day's work, even for the most experienced horses. Then build up according to the individual. If things are going well, it takes little time to get a horse working at around the height at which you want to finish up. But if a horse gets an unnecessary fright, you will more likely spend double that time putting the job right again and getting his confidence back. It is therefore better to err on the side of caution.

Most horses tend to exhaust themselves far more quickly if left to their own devices than ever they will when taking advice from the saddle. So never let a horse carry on with this sort of work to the point of exhaustion or

This mare was one individual who certainly benefited from a little jumping work either on the lunge or loose. She had a lot of ability and was a great trier but was over-bold, had a bad technique (she carried her head very high into a fence) and occasionally left one or both front legs down. If anyone described such a horse to me, I wouldn't drive round the corner to see it. But this one was different – she did in fact win a lot of classes. This photograph is typical of her. She has run in deep and has obviously had to put in a lot of effort to avoid hitting the fence in front. In spite of that her forelegs are still too low.

There are several points in favour of free-jumping the horse like this. It teaches him, when running into trouble, to look after himself and to think for himself. If a horse is always ridden to fences, the rider will tend to do a little too much to rectify the situation from the saddle. It's less wearing to stand on the ground and let a horse educate himself a little, than it is to sit up there arguing the toss with a headstrong individual as to how it's best to jump a fence.

It can do no harm to teach any horse to back off a fence and think for himself, as opposed to supporting his front end with the hand. That will merely make him more dependent on the rider instead of concentrating on jumping that top rail himself. I'm convinced that it simply doesn't make sense, at least in training, to support a horse with the hand and to fabricate a jump. Of course, in competition, and especially in a tight corner when setting about trying to win a class, I'd be the first to support a horse in any way I could. But in training it's always best to go back to the drawing board and teach a horse to jump correctly and to do the lion's share of the job himself.

I prefer to work all my horses on the flat and try to achieve the shape and outline I want with hands and heels alone. However, sometimes I do get an awkward customer who benefits from being driven. It's very rewarding to see how a horse who can be a demon to ride, and who tends to meet the rider head on, will give himself to the situation when being driven. After a few sessions on the long reins most horses are more supple, softer to the hand and tractable to ride.

breathlessness. Pull up frequently, watch for heaving sides, listen to his breathing and avoid, at all costs a fatigued horse going back to his box in a muck sweat.

What is not done today can in most cases be left until tomorrow.

Lungeing on the Flat and Over Fences
As a general rule, once a horse has passed his early educational training I do not do a lot of work on the lunge (as I explained in Chapter 2, the one area where I do tend to use the lunge a good deal is in the education of riders). However, constructive work can be done by lungeing both on the flat and over various fences, and from time to time I find that the odd horse benefits from being worked from the ground rather than from the saddle.

Some riders make a habit of always putting hot, gassy horses on the lunge for half an hour or more before riding them, simply to take the steam out of them and to make them concentrate more on the immediate work in hand. That is fine – though I do wish that some grooms would choose a better place to lunge a horse than a crowded collecting ring, where they prevent riders from working and sometimes cause horses to bump into or shy away from each other.

An impetuous horse, who rushes his fences, and consequently becomes long and flat, will often benefit from jogging quietly round on the lunge in trot and popping over a small fence or combination of poles, simply designed to shorten him and get his shoulders in the air. It is no bad plan on occasions to lunge a horse over fences at home as part of his training, particularly one who tends to be a little over-bold and incautious. Left to their own devices, horses tend, if they have enough commonsense, to learn quickly to put themselves right and to shorten their stride. Running themselves into a few fences very often shortens them more quickly than if they are taught from the saddle, although a combination of the two methods would be ideal. If a horse continually runs into fences and hits them in front or behind, he is unlikely to make a show jumper anyway.

In the case of a horse with a high head carriage, or bad muscular development in the neck, good results can also be achieved by lungeing for short periods with the aid of a Chambon.

LIBRARY
BISHOP BURTON COLLEGE
BEVERLEY HU17 8QG

CHAPTER 7

Technique

When I set out to organise the photographs to accompany this chapter I chose two horses who happened to be in the yard at the time and who were as far removed from each other in technique as they could possibly be. I felt that I needed one horse who, in my opinion, had a really good technique, so that the photographs would give an overall impression of what I am trying to say. I also thought it necessary to find a horse with a poor technique to illustrate the huge gap that exists between a natural show jumper and a horse who, through no fault of his own, was not born with the same talent.

The grey horse in this chapter, who also played such a big part in the flat work sequences in Chapter 3, is an Irish-bred seven-year-old and a really nice individual. Although he is a great mover he just missed as a show jumper because his technique made the business hard for him and, unfortunately, he is also not blessed with an abundance of courage. He won through his Newcomers classes as easily as shelling peas, but then struggled through Foxhunter and Grade C onwards and I sold him for a reasonable price to a young lady from Lancashire to ride at club level, in working hunter classes and at unaffiliated shows. Thanks to the drop in class, he is a lot happier and is performing well. I am very happy to say that the customer is delighted.

The brown mare, who was pictured in the before-and-after sequence in Chapter 1, is, I hope, a different story. Again Irish bred, she came to England as a four-year-old, and was six when these photographs were taken. At the time of writing she was in her first serious season, winning nice competitions regularly. She is fortunate enough to have been born with a really good technique which means that jumping comes easily to her. She is brave and careful enough and has a big jump. With a bit of luck she should go a long way. It is difficult at this stage to assess just how far a horse will go, but I would be disappointed if this one were not good enough to jump at Grade A level.

Young horses are always a gamble; some turn out far

better than one expects, the majority far worse. That reminds me of a story which was told to me at an Irish dinner party by Northern Ireland international rider and dealer Tommy Vance. One day Tommy was invited by his pal Eddie Macken to drive south to look at a horse which Eddie had on price. Because the price was quite substantial, he wanted to go back and have a second look. Eddie said that in any case it might be worth Tommy's while because there was a mare not far from there that he might find useful for a customer.

Eddie's brown horse could do nothing right that day and in Tommy's words 'went diabolical' so, getting into the car, the two riders drove to the next place to look at a six-year-old chestnut mare standing about 16hh. She had been jumped around small classes for a couple of years in the south of Ireland, but for one reason or another Tommy did not buy her. The two men drove home. It is not an unusual story. I have often done the same myself, and spent several days looking at horses only to buy a fraction of the number I wanted. The sequel to this story is that the brown horse whom Eddie was trying turned out to be Preachan, who jumped so successfully for Graham Fletcher and Geoff Billington. The chestnut was none other than Jessica, the incredible little mare who carried Switzerland's Heidi Robbiani to so many successes at Grand Prix level.

That story is typical of how things turn out with horses and there can hardly be any top rider who does not have his own personal anecdote along similar lines. Some horses improve with age, others never get past a certain point, while others again fail to live up to early promise. I would never buy a horse of any description who did not jump in an orthodox way with what is generally accepted as good show jumping technique. The two horses pictured on page 114 should, I hope, illustrate what I mean – even in these two opening shots. To my mind the two photographs show a near perfect example of one horse jumping round and the other jumping hollow. The brown mare is doing just about everything right in order to clear this little open water ditch: she is getting her head down and her shoulders well up and snapping her front legs away in super style. If you study this photograph you can see why some horses who are really good in front sometimes puncture their own chests with their studs and have to wear a protective leather chestguard. I would always be a customer for a youngster who does this. It is not difficult to imagine the sort of feel this one gives you when she leaves the ground. That lovely sensation when the withers come up and hit you in the chest is very apparent here. All I have to do is

Left: A perfect example of a horse jumping with a round outline.
Below: An equally good example of a horse jumping hollow.

just sit quietly and follow the movement, because she is so trustworthy when it comes to leaving fences up. You can always come from a long way out and trust her to jump that top rail. Having got her bowling along, you can literally go from start to finish round a course at one pace and just allow her own natural rhythm and ability to look after the fences.

Unfortunately the same could never be said for the grey horse. I hate to criticise him really, but some unfortunate animal has to get it in the neck to illustrate the point, and he, poor fellow, happened to be the one who was around on the day that Kit Houghton, the photographer, arrived. He is doing most things wrong here: just compare his head and neck and the position of his shoulders with the horse in the other photograph and you will see what I mean. He often jumped with his head in the air, which was quite a paradox considering how super he was in his flat work. It was because he was so good at that aspect that he was given the job when the flat work photographic sequence was being put together.

In this photograph you can see that he has dried up on me a little. Instead of his head and neck going down and away from me and his shoulders coming up, the reverse has happened. His shoulders are staying down and going straight on and his head is coming back at me. Because of his hesitation he has tended to throw my body weight forward a little. He also seems to be scrambling over the fence because his front legs are just anyhow, and certainly not a pair as the mare's are in the other photograph.

Incidentally I always felt that this grey horse would have made an ideal eventer. His flat work, as I have said, is excellent and he is – like so many other horses who do not find show jumping easy – really terrific across country. Although he had reached his own ceiling in show jumping, it would have been quite passable for an eventer. It did not work out that way, but at least he has a good home and is making one young rider very happy.

To illustrate the capabilities of the two horses, I set up a small double of parallels with one non-jumping stride in between. It is not often that you see a double of parallels in novice classes, but from a schooling point of view, as long as they are not over-big and wide, a double of square spreads with a short stride between has a lot of advantages.

This was obviously a satisfactory approach, as can be seen from my attitude. I'm sitting about where I'd want to be and am not defending in any way. Evidently I feel that there's no danger of hitting this fence because my eye is already weighing up the second part of the double. My hands are relaxed, which suggests that I was happy with the pace on the approach; I'm simply content to go along with things as they are.

I think this is an outstanding shot, and one which certainly flatters the rider – but then it isn't often that you have the opportunity to pose for a jumping photo. Quite honestly, who couldn't pretend to look good on one that jumps like this? The picture says it all. The mare is doing everything right: a perfect round jump, using herself in every way and getting a lot of height. If this fence had been a foot higher and wider, she'd have jumped it just as easily. Obviously, with the co-operation I'm getting, I'm still concentrating on the next part of the double. I'm getting well forward and following the movement of her head and neck. At this stage it would be unwise to sit back and slip the reins because, with another fence one short stride away and with the mare jumping in so strongly, I may well want to shorten her before the next.

Here the mare is making an excellent job of following through and using her hind legs. Just look at her ability to bend her hocks. She's obviously just about to give a reassuring flick of the tail, which I love to see in a jumper. I still have a nice contact, which isn't difficult on a horse like this because her jump is so predictable. It isn't difficult to sit in a good position throughout a sequence of fences because it's so easy to anticipate her every move.

This photograph shows why horses with short, upright pasterns don't stay sound for very long. See how the mare's pastern is operating as a shock absorber: the foot looks as if it's quite literally parted from the leg. It's interesting to note the mare's expression. Most horses who really try to jump fences are more often than not caught with their ears back, through deep concentration, but here the one fence is forgotten and she's looking cheerfully to the next part. This picture also shows the value of overreach and tendon boots, for with the near fore in that position it would be very simple for it to be struck into from behind. Prevention is certainly better than cure.

One down and one to go: things have gone so well at the first part that I simply have to go along with her and give her a little squeeze to move to the second part. When jumping doubles and trebles it's important to train a horse to jump in well, otherwise he'll find it more difficult to jump. Here the mare has gone in so soundly that the second part is going to be very simple, too. However, she's so much on my terms that if I wanted to lengthen or shorten at this point it would be very easy to do so.

The position of my hands suggests that I might be tempted to pull her off that front rail, but the slight loop in the rein tells me that I'm not. I think there's little point in supporting the horse at a fence with the hand. If horses consistently need lifting over fences with the hand, they become so dependent upon it that they eventually pack up thinking for themselves and need rider support for ever more. Let the horse do the jumping: it's the rider's job to get him to the fence from the best possible approach, but from that point on it's all down to the horse.

Ears back again, and a tremendous thrust off the ground. She hasn't folded her front legs as neatly here as in the other photographs but, in fairness, she's getting so much height that she hardly needs to. As this is the second part of the double, I suppose that I have a slight excuse for looking down, but basically I feel it's always better to look straight ahead and start planning the next turn or fence or change of direction. It's too late now for me to do anything about this particular fence so there's little point in looking at it.

This photograph illustrates just how happy the mare is to accept a light contact throughout the jump, though I could have a loop in the rein and it really wouldn't make any difference to her performance. There's a lovely feeling of power about this frame. She's bounded up in the air and is making it look very simple indeed which to her, with the fences at this height, it certainly is.

It's always difficult to predict just how far a horse is going to go – there are so many qualities needed by the show jumper to make a complete picture. A technique such as this mare possesses is a great asset because years of training would never produce this kind of jump from a horse who didn't have it. It's not surprising that good show jumpers are so expensive when real talent is comparatively rare.

Poor Russell – he's about to get another ear-bashing! Honestly, I did like him really, but I had to pick on somebody. Here, in spite of what I remember as quite a decent approach, he's spooking at the first part of the double and is obviously worrying about the second. His hesitation has thrown me off balance and my expression and white-knuckled grip on the reins tell the world that things aren't right. This sequence wasn't stage-managed – I just had an idea that he'd give me the shots I was looking for.

Oh dear, now we're in trouble! He's still backing off and looking a bit sceptical about the whole thing. While trying not to hang him too badly in the mouth, I have nevertheless adopted the safety seat and, teeth gritted, prepared for what might be the worst at the next fence. He's jumping very hollow backed and drawing his hind legs underneath him, nearly taking the front rail with him in the process. He's already losing distance and giving the impression that he could quite easily land on the back rail, which would stop him dead in his tracks before the next part.

Panic stations: having landed short, that back rail now looks a long way off and I have to do something about it quickly. So, sitting down, I'm giving him a kick and a squeeze to get him as close up to the front rail as possible. From the look on his face and the position of his ears he's obviously doubtful, but I'm committed now and there's no turning back.

Well, we got there, but it's a bit of a scramble and neither of us looks really happy. He's a bit far off and is doubtless going to have to reach for that back rail. Again, a better technique and rounder jump would have helped; throwing his head and neck back is certainly not helping him to make up distance.

In fairness, he's making quite a brave stab at this and is at least starting to dip his head a little. However, his hind legs show just how much tension there is through his body, and the fact that I'm still sitting a little bit behind him shows that there's doubt in my mind, too. This parallel is fairly typical of one that I'd build at home. I don't believe in making them too simple for a horse who has had some experience, and would quite often build a fence like this without a ground line. I also prefer a parallel to be really square to make the horse work a little.

The previous picture has shown how unhappy I seemed with the situation – this picture proves it. I wouldn't have wanted this fence to have been much higher or wider. Russell looks quite happy about things now that it's all over but, while he didn't have this fence down, as the picture clearly shows he wasn't far from sitting in the middle of it. That does no horse any good, particularly a reluctant one. Next time he might think twice about coming at all.

The Water Jump

A horse's ability to take water jumps and ditches in his stride can make all the difference between success and failure – even at local show level. It makes sense to school the young horse from quite an early age to take the unusual type of obstacle in his stride, as if it were no more difficult than any other fence – which, with proper training, it should not prove to be. How often one sees a novice lose his chance of a shot at the Foxhunter final at Wembley by blowing it at the water in his regional final.

If a horse has been well hunted, or has done some hunter trials or eventing, he should make the transition to show jumping comparatively easily. If, on the other hand, he has only ever met a standard set of show jumps, the job is a little more difficult. As in ordinary schooling over fences, horses thrive on confidence. It therefore follows that it is wise to take one stage at a time and not ask for too much too soon. In novice competition it is rare to find a water of more than 12ft, but without adequate preparation even this can be a formidable obstacle for a novice. He may well go and jump it in innocence the first time. But come back again when he knows it is there, and it can be a very different story.

I have two permanent water jumps at home, one about 10ft wide and the other only 4ft. The latter also serves as a water ditch to be used under various other fences. I always start horses over the small one. When a horse has been working in the jumping paddock he should be quite used to seeing the water just from being trotted and cantered about in his normal warming-up routine work. I put the water jump brush (well sloped) on the very edge of the water, making for as little spread as possible, and also put a rustic pole a couple of feet high directly over the water. This tends to make a horse concentrate more on the pole than on the water. In fact, with the brush and pole, and only about 5ft of spread, he can see very little water anyway. Having jumped a variety of other fences until I am satisfied that he is going well into the bridle and jumping fluently, I then canter straight on and jump the little water as if it were just any other fence, though perhaps with a little more pace and certainly plenty of support from the leg and reasonably firm contact with the hand. I find that very few horses have any hesitation in going first time.

I then give him a pat and a few words of encouragement and immediately bring him again and repeat the exercise. After four or five jumps he should be taking little notice of the water and taking the fence in his stride. At this stage it is a good idea to leave him for that day. Repeat the process next day and, if all goes well, the next stage is to remove the pole and come again. If by now the horse is showing no signs of anxiety, it is possible to pull the brush out a foot or so and gradually to work away until he is confidently jumping about 6ft or 7ft of water.

Next day follow the same process. Then it is time to tackle the big water. I always put the brush into the water, but with no water showing on the take-off edge; again, put a pole about 3ft high over the centre. From now on it is largely down to the individual horse as to how far one goes at each session, but with care he should very soon be jumping a full 10ft or so without the pole.

When training over water, never allow a horse to jump low, or he will soon be aiming at the tape. A water with a pole over it, set about 3ft or 4ft from the ground, encourages a horse to get plenty of height, an essential factor if he is to become a good water jumper. The better your water jump, the better the water jumpers you will produce. It is a long-held belief amongst people who know their business that the blame for Britain traditionally producing bad water jumpers could be laid squarely on the shoulders of the bad water jumps which at one time were a

The first thing to bear in mind when jumping water is that it's essential really to have the horse going somewhere from a long way out. If you have a lot of room in which to set the horse up, move him up a gear or two from plenty far back and teach him from the outset to attack. There's never any percentage in jumping water defensively.

I believe that the technique involved in jumping water is different from that of any other fence. At a water jump you get the horse going first, then adjust the stride; at any other single fence the first objective is to adjust the stride and then move the horse forward into the fence. Here, because I have plenty of movement, I'm just taking a little check to put the mare right. This isn't going to cost anything because we have plenty of impulsion and I can pick up a stride, be it longer or shorter, out of that pace. The water is one fence where you can happily mix pace and impulsion.

Having made the required adjustment, I can now kick on again and try to get her right up to the brush. There are no faults for knocking the brush down, so the closer you can get to it the better and the more likely you are to clear the business end, the tape. The mare is obviously now committed to the fence and her near fore and off hind show how she's lengthened her stride.

Having got sufficient pace and the stride I wanted, all I need do now is to sit still, squeeze and drive forward, and not get over the point of balance but rather sit a fraction behind the movement, allowing the shoulders to come up. At water, height is almost as important as width.

The mare is obviously getting plenty of height and her hindquarters suggest that there's plenty of width to come. More often than not I have a pole over the water at home, even with experienced horses, since I feel that at all times horses should be encouraged to stay up in the air. You'll notice that I've put an extra pair of wings at this fence to help keep the horse in the middle and to have something to aim at. Because you have so much pace it's important, particularly with a young horse, to keep him straight and running right to the centre of the fence. The rails at the side are an added incentive to keep straight. Many inexperienced water jumpers have a tendency to panic a little and run down the fence to one side or the other. In your own paddock you can at least arrange to have everything in your favour.

The end product: a happy horse, with a good expression, throwing a bold, confident jump and allowing the rider to sit in a comfortable position and not worry about landing in the water. From early lessons such as this, you could happily progress to removing the pole and/or pulling the brush back a few feet, according to how wide you want to jump bearing in mind the horse's experience. A horse who's been well schooled at home will invariably get more height and width in competition over a strange fence.

regular feature of a lot of county-level shows. We have traditionally lagged behind our European competitors where water jumping is concerned mainly because Continental water jumps are better constructed and therefore produce better water jumpers.

Ditches

Having got the water-jump technique safely under his belt, it is now time for the horse to move on to the dry ditch. Again, start very small and have a nice inviting fence of rustic poles built over it. There is no need to have a great gaping hole for a ditch; for schooling purposes just taking the turf off and exposing the earth below is quite sufficient in the early stages. It is amazing what a difference it makes digging the shallowest of ditches under a fence. Alternatively, it is not difficult to build your own portable water trays which, painted a bright colour such as white or blue, will have the same desired effect as most permanent obstacles.

The same riding technique applies, but do try not to be too ambitious too soon, and always encourage the youngster to enjoy himself. Over a period of time you should have your horse jumping the water and ditches with confidence and treating them the same as any other obstacles. From then on it should be plain sailing.

It is both constructive and enjoyable to experiment with other fences on the water and ditch theme. With ditches, be a little adventurous. A parallel bar above a ditch is a fence often encountered, as is a ditch with vertical poles behind it. When a young horse has mastered all the unusual fences he is likely to meet in competition, not only is he a more complete show jumper but also his knowledge will work in his favour. He will be able to jump difficult obstacles with confidence while other, less educated horses are making disastrous mistakes. It is well worth taking the trouble to teach him his job.

CHAPTER 8

Going to Shows

I believe that it is a good plan to let a horse win through his grades in his own time, and accordingly jump in the lowest grade that his money winnings will allow. If he is a decent horse, he will be upgraded soon enough. If there happens to be a clear round or non-affiliated section at a show, take advantage of the chance to have a school round in public and then later on jump in the Newcomers or Pathfinders. It was a good decision on the part of the BSJA to move the Newcomers final to Wembley so that even the beginner has an objective for the season and does not have to take on the now quite strong and competitive Foxhunter competitions.

The Season's Programme
When mapping out a season for one or more horses, it is often a good policy to pick on one focal point of the season and work backwards from that time, in much the same way that a top rider would plan his campaign around his best horse's preparation for a European or World Championship, or Olympic Games. The strategy is just the same, even if you only have in mind the possibility of qualifying for the Newcomers or Foxhunter final at Wembley, or at least making the Regional Finals of those competitions, which usually fall in the same summer.

Horses cannot go all the year round, year in and year out. They need a break, just as humans do. Whether a horse is given short breaks often or a whole winter off from September to March – give or take a month – depends on the rider's circumstances: how much he wants to do, when he wants to do it (i.e. the indoor winter circuit or the outdoor summer circuit) and any particular objective he may have in mind. I personally have become a little bit bored with the winter circuit. Having done it for many years I no longer enjoy standing around in the freezing cold, and I far prefer to revolve my season around the summer. But perhaps a compromise would be the best solution.

If a horse has not qualified for Wembley, and the plan is

not to jump throughout the winter, it is sometimes a good idea to rough him off during September (when there is still a little grass and some summer days left) and to let him enjoy two or three months complete break, out day and night, until the bad weather arrives around Christmas. At that time I generally bring all my horses in at night and then possibly begin fittening work, followed by serious work around February to March, when it is possible to open up a new season for a horse by taking in a few shows on the late winter indoor circuit. Since most people seem to have the same idea, it is certainly the hardest time of the year to win classes – but then you are never going to win your fortune on the local indoor circuit. In any case, if everyone viewed show jumping as a way of making a fortune, we should soon all be out of a job.

The beauty of starting early and with a mid-summer or autumn objective in mind is that you can always choose to give the horse a mini-break of perhaps two weeks at some point during the season. A good time might be during one of those long, hot spells which we sometimes have around July and August, when the ground is so bone hard that it does more harm than good to jump a horse. If the weather is really hot, I try to turn my horses out at first light – we start around six in the morning anyway in summer – and then bring them in again in the late morning so that they are not driven half crazy by flies. Or, alternatively, if the weather is really warm they can be turned out completely but possibly brought in for a few hours during the heat of the day when the flies are most troublesome. With just a short break like that they do not usually become too unfit and can be picked up to show condition again in a matter of days.

Some horses are better suited to indoor shows, especially older ones who may be a little short of wind and cannot cope with really long outdoor courses, or those who have perhaps had several seasons wear-and-tear on the circuit and now prefer a bit of give in the going. These horses can have the summer off and can be brought back into work in time to be firing on all cylinders when the indoor season starts in the autumn.

There are certainly enough shows nowadays to keep a string of horses employed on the indoor circuit. However, unless a horse is of high enough calibre to be travelling to CSIs abroad and on the highly lucrative World Cup circuit, the whole winter exercise is best regarded as an educational time for horses or to prepare them for sale.

Travelling

There are many different ways of transporting horses to competitions, from the lowliest single trailer towed behind the family car to the luxury six-stall horsebox with living accommodation – complete with showers, toilets and every other amenity which you would expect to find in an average family home (and costing about the same). Whichever method of transport you use to take your horse to a show, it will have no bearing on how successful he is when he gets there – provided he has been comfortably loaded in a roomy stall and sympathetically driven to the showground. Certainly it is nice to enjoy the comforts of a luxury horsebox, but as far as competition is concerned it is what walks down the ramp that counts.

Fashions in horseboxes change over the years, but it is now generally accepted that the ideal way to travel horses is diagonally across the lorry. Whether it is the horses' heads or quarters that face the front depends on personal preference and the geography of the lorry, taking into account the living accommodation. But it is a fact that if you turn a horse loose to travel in a lorry he will always stand diagonally of his own accord. The amount of space needed between the partitions largely depends on the individual. It is not just a question of a horse's size, but also of the room he needs to spread his legs and brace himself on corners. Some horses are naturally good travellers, others are bad and never really become used to it. It is the same as with people – if you travel badly, no matter what you try it never seems to get better. So if you have a horse who suffers discomfort on the road, you have to make life as easy as possible for him.

The most common problem is when horses fall about on corners. They will actually scramble, lose their legs and go down in the lorry if they are not given the room they need. I have seen this happen many times in double trailers, when horses of any size seem to be cooped and cramped. Removing the middle partition and giving one horse, however big, both stalls will certainly cure the problem. Alternatively, move the back end of the partition over to the wall of the trailer, thus allowing the horse to spread his hind legs and brace himself on corners; when he no longer panics around corners, the problem is solved.

I am not a believer in the full-length partitions which are used almost exclusively in racehorse transporters. They are too claustrophobic, and though they might be all right for small racehorses, a box load of big strapping show jumpers travel like sardines. Many riders these days are changing to a single bar – strong enough to take a horse's weight – between each horse, and below that about 3ft or 4ft of stout rubber matting, which allows horses to spread their legs but not to kick their neighbours. The most important thing of all is to have headboards to stop them getting at each other. To have a team of jumpers who all get on with each other without argument is very nearly impossible. While some horses, like people, are inoffensive and even-tempered, in every team there is sure to be one hellraiser who gets on with nobody else. Headboards to prevent them snarling at each other are the answer to all that.

I am not very fond of hay and straw in lorries. Straw is too messy – it gets in the horses' tails and over their rugs and generally blows everywhere, making the place untidy. I give my horses haynets to come home with, but by that stage of the day the outfit is not quite so tidy as when it set out, so I am quite prepared to put up with a few hayseeds

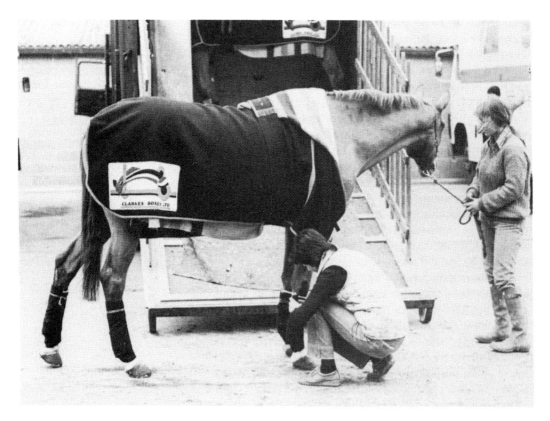

Clothing is obviously dictated by the time of the season. This photograph was taken on a late winter's day at Stoneleigh and the clipped-out horses still needed a blanket. I always use a length of carpet on the back ramp to save wear and tear on the coconut matting and the slats. With back ramp only lorries the ramp does undergo an exceptional amount of wear and tear – better to tear up an old piece of carpet.

about the place. Like most show jumpers, I travel my horses on rubber mats. The type used in milking parlours are very strong, as they are made of inch-thick, hard rubber. Although they cost a lot they last for ever. They are easily cut to size and will go down in a lorry like fitted carpet. On top of the mats I use a thin layer of sawdust or shavings to soak up the moisture and droppings. A brush and shovel should always be kept in the lorry so that it can be mucked out at intervals during a long day.

It is worth mentioning the disposal of the muckings-out from a lorry on show days. If it is a summer show, no farmer is going to object if people throw droppings out on to his field. But do be considerate at indoor shows in the winter. It is no joke for owners of indoor establishments to find their once tidy lorry park smothered with droppings, shavings and straw after a show.

Like most people, I always travel my horses in Gamgee tissue and bandages to protect their legs, though I do not use knee pads or hock boots. When horses travel diagonally I find that they do not scrape their hocks, and in the event of an accident they would fall sideways, not on their knees.

What to Take

There is no end to the gear required for a day's show jumping, and it seems that whether you have one horse or six, the amount you have to take along is nearly the same. The rider needs roughly the same equipment whether he is going to ride one horse or several. Where the horses are concerned, I rarely take duplicates of anything because in the event of breakages I can always borrow a martingale, noseband, stirrup leather or rein from another horse's tack. I do not believe in cluttering the lorry with unnecessary gear.

Essential items fall into two categories: those that live in the lorry permanently and those which are taken on in the morning and off-loaded again at night. I keep my own riding wear permanently in the wardrobe in the lorry. Without having to worry about jackets, riding hat and boots (both rubber and leather), I then only have to check that a white shirt and tie and two pairs of breeches come out of the house along with the food basket (I am not very fond of showground food and always prefer to take my own and dip into it whenever time allows during the day). I always take a spare pair of breeches. Constant washing wears white breeches out faster than anything, and seams, zips and buttons seem to fall apart with monotonous regularity. Buttons for tweed and red jackets, plus the appropriate thread and needles, never leave the lorry. Some riders are lucky with buttons on jackets – I am one of those unfortunate people who seems to lose one a day.

Perhaps the most important items, other than your regular riding gear, are waterproofs for both rider and horses. Summers vary a lot, but it is a safe bet that during a season everybody concerned is going to get several severe drenchings. Waterproof rugs, which cover the horse literally from his ears to his tail, are ideal and must be complete with fillet strings to go under the tail and neck to prevent the rugs from departing across the showground in high winds. There are any number of waterproof outfits for riders, ranging from full-length macs with big collars and with enough length to come halfway between the knee and the ground, to waterproof over-breeches and three-quarter length jackets to match. I prefer the latter because I do not like big skirts on macs flapping about and distracting horses.

Some fabrics are noisier than others and can disturb a horse. I clearly remember a couple of years ago taking the Young Riders team to Donaueschingen in West Germany. On a torrentially wet Nations Cup day Janet Hunter was having all sorts of problems in getting the explosive Lisnamarrow to settle at the practice fence. In desperation I suggested she took off her mac, which was blowing about in the howling wind. The horse settled immediately and, ever since, I have been less inclined to use those otherwise excellent Australian-style full-length macs. I prefer a three-quarter length waxed coat which will resist any amount of rain. Quilted jackets are fine for frosty days but are generally worse than useless in the wet.

I often wear gloves as a matter of course when riding, but in any case they are a great asset on a wet day, when reins are slippy and a horse is taking a strong hold. I prefer thin leather, and find that the best of all are Canadian rawhide gloves which cowboys use in cattle-roping contests. I used to have them brought back by friends who had been to Calgary show, but I have recently seen them on sale in tack shops in this country.

While on the subject of leather, a pair of chaps is a very useful garment. I never use them at day shows but find them ideal for exercising horses both at home and at staying-away shows. They can be quickly zipped over a pair of jeans and boots. In fact I now take chaps with me on horse-buying expeditions, as it certainly saves either wandering round in breeches and boots all day or constant changes of clothes, something which is not always convenient. What is more, they are very warm in winter, providing as they do an extra layer. I find them a great comfort on a frosty morning in an indoor school.

I am not much in favour of rubber riding boots because I far prefer the feel and support of a well-made pair of leather boots. But on wet days I certainly prefer them. They are easy to clean and they save your best boots from becoming prematurely worn out by bad weather.

It makes life a lot easier if each horse has his own individual set of tack, including tendon and overreach boots, and if possible his own saddle, so that you do not have to rush about changing tack in the happy event of having more than one horse in a jump-off. I always keep a variety of cooling rugs and sweat sheets, as well as a few warm blankets, in the show skip and lorry.

Over the years I have, like many other riders, collected a great variety of bits. These always live in a wooden box in the lorry. When I am at home I know exactly where they are, and at a show I always have them to hand. It seems that the majority of them are never used but, as with so many unworn items in a wardrobe, I can never bring myself to part with them. Anyway, it is useful to have a nucleus of bits to hand at a show. Certain horses need a frequent change of bit and I am quite likely to change bits between classes or even, in some instances, between the first round and the jump-off. A leather punch lives in the same box. Quite frequently, holes need to be punched in some items of leather on a show day. Two or three spare headcollar ropes also live in the skip. I tend to tie horses to the side of the lorry for tacking up, studding and grooming, and it is not unusual for a horse to run back and break a rope or stand on it and do likewise. Attaching a loop of string to the tying-up ring and tying the horse to that helps to prevent such breakages.

A general-purpose medicine box for both horses and humans is always useful to have around and should include such things as plasters, bandages, antiseptics, wound sprays, as well as electrolyte powders for use during long journeys, especially by boat, or B12 injections which may be necessary during long, arduous shows. In summer a fly repellant of some sort is essential.

I always offer the horses a drink of water immediately after their class and again before setting off for home. Taps can be difficult to find at some shows, so it is best to take you own water with you. I also like, whenever possible, to give a horse a bite of grass at a show after the competition. It is relaxing and breaks up the day; anything which makes a day's jumping more enjoyable for a horse must be beneficial. A haynet for the journey home is usually adequate. But if the horses are away from early morning to quite late at night – as they can be when there are novices and Grade As on the same lorry – I occasionally give them a small feed at some stage. However, with the exception of the early morning feed, I am not really in favour of stuffing a horse with food before he jumps.

The girls usually have their own individual grooming kits and simply have to load them on the lorry in the morning, making sure that they have such things as rubber bands or needle and thread for plaiting, tack cleaning kit, and so on. Shoe polish, brushes and a clothes brush live permanently in the lorry.

Generally, loading the horses at home is the very last job before leaving. I find that a gang of fresh horses first thing in the morning can be a bit of a pain when they start arguing and battering the lorry before the day has begun. For that reason, the last task before setting off is all hands on deck, a horse apiece, load them, ramp up and away.

Arriving at the Show/Warming Up
I like whenever possible to allow time for the horses to rest for a little while when they arrive at a show. Having been in the lorry for an hour or two, they should be settled enough to stand quietly and compose themselves ready for work. Their minds at that time should be a little more on the job than when they left home.

Unload the horse in plenty of time before his class and, again, let him settle. A really green novice will benefit from walking round the showground for at least half an hour and if possible being taken all around the outside of the ring where he can view it from every angle. This will enable him to become accustomed to the distractions of the showground before he actually takes his turn in the ring.

I try to do my working-in away from the main collecting ring, which always seems to be too congested. The amount of work each horse requires before a class varies enormously. A highly strung novice may need up to an hour of quiet work to put him together, while an old Grade A, who knows the business, merely needs a walk around for a time, a few canters in circles and half a dozen little jumps before going in. If there is only the practice ring in which to work, be considerate to other competitors and, with luck, they will be the same to you. It is in everyone's interests to keep out of each other's way and to be as little nuisance to other riders as possible. As I have already mentioned, one thing which annoys me intensely is grooms endlessly lungeing horses in a corner of the practice ring, which disrupts everything.

Time your warming-up period as accurately as possible. Depending on how long it is taking for each horse to jump, I usually like to have a practice jump when I am about eight or nine away from my turn. Much less and the horse is breathless when he goes in; much more and he has forgotten what he has just done or has gone off the boil. With some horses it pays to have one more jump a minute or so before you go in, just to make sure that his mind is on the job. Then let him settle and think about what he is doing.

The unwritten law at the practice fence is that in any argument as to who should have the use of it, the rider who is nearest to his turn has first call. There is nothing to be gained by arguing the toss with a fellow competitor. Even in quite small competitions riders can become a bit uptight and tempers quickly become frayed. A polite, easy-going attitude at a relatively difficult time makes the day go more easily.

Just as at home, I normally start, if things are not too hectic in there, by trotting over a couple of crossed poles or small verticals and then work up, perhaps over three or four canter jumps, to a vertical fence about the height of those in the ring. I can never see the sense in the tactics employed by a minority of riders who habitually seem to jump 1ft higher and 2ft wider than they will have to where it matters. It is so much wasted effort and burns horses out long before their time. Granted, the odd horse might on occasions need a biggish fence to get him up in the air, to attract his attention and to make him try that bit harder. But I certainly do not think that it is a good idea to make it a way of life.

If things are going well at the vertical, perhaps the next step would be to move to a small parallel – most shows have two practice fences these days. Again, build up to the height of fence that the horse will meet in the ring. If all has gone well, there should now be time to jump off him for a couple of minutes, perhaps pull the saddle forward (a lifelong habit of mine – in fact I have given up trying to cure myself of that one) but, more importantly, just let him settle, relax and have a breather before switching him on again ready for action.

When to Go

At most small shows the order of jumping is decided simply by riders putting their names down on a blackboard. Do not go too early in the class – about three-quarters of the way down the list is a good place if you have just one horse. That way he will get a breather before the jump-off but, more important, it gives the rider time to watch a number of horses go and to observe in detail the course being ridden. If you have two horses, and assuming there are thirty to forty horses in the class, it might be a good idea to go about a quarter of the way down on the first horse, which still gives you a chance to watch one or two competitors go before you have a practice jump on that one. It also gives you a slight breather and time to jump the other one before he takes his turn towards the end. If there are not many horses in the class and you have two rides, one or both of the horses will need to have been given sufficient work beforehand.

Walking the Course
It is easier said than done, but walking the course is a job best undertaken alone and with your mind clearly on the decisions you have to make, as opposed to strolling round with a few friends having a bit of chatter. There is more to it than simply learning which way you have to go. The variations in fences, distances and direction are the important factors. It is certainly a big advantage to know whether between certain fences you will need to ride strongly, to sit still and wait for the fence to come to you, or to hold the horse up and try to get in an extra stride. Try to assess the danger areas of a course and how they are likely to affect the horse that you are riding. For example, in the case of a really green horse, it is odds on that his biggest problem will be at a double. With experience, such problems become obvious to a rider.

Learn to step out distances between fences, not only in doubles and trebles but also related distances between other fences as well – for example, at fences more than two but less than five strides apart. If you are in doubt about how to ride a line of fences or how to walk a combination fence, do not hesitate to ask an experienced rider. He will not bite your head off and will, I am sure, be only too pleased to come up with a bit of advice. Yes, really – we all like to have our opinion asked, don't we?

Fences obviously fall into two main categories, verticals and spreads, and broadly speaking one could say that a spread requires a more powerful approach than a vertical and, conversely, that a vertical requires more precision than a spread.

As a general rule the course designer (ostensibly a competent and knowledgeable person) will do his best to build a course which encourages the horse to take on the fences at a level pace and educates him in readiness for the

day when he takes on the best at top level. The one basic ingredient which every horse needs injecting into him, in large and regular doses, is confidence. Show jumping standards seem to become higher every year and a horse should never be left in any doubt as to whether he is able to cope with what is being asked of him. The rider's contribution to this mental attitude is to minimise the amount of times during his education that the young horse is given a fright or an unpleasant experience. It is for this reason that, when walking a course, the rider needs to develop the instinct of knowing which fences are relatively simple and can be jumped in a relaxed (not casual) manner and, more important, sensing the potential trouble spots.

Distances and dimensions obviously play a big part in a rider's calculations when walking a course. The bigger the course, the more accurate a rider has to be in planning the way he will ride certain fences and distances. There is no margin for error at top level. But at local level, too, plans still have to be made. It is just as important for novice horses and riders to get it right as it is for the others. A little forethought and intelligent appraisal of how to ride different sections of the course will certainly pay dividends.

Train yourself to measure distances at home by pacing out doubles, trebles and related distances between two or more fences. Assess how each distance will ride, then get on board and ride it and see if you were right. If you make a few mistakes, it will soon sharpen up your judgement of distance and pace.

If you are one of the first to go you must have a clear plan in mind of how to ride a line of fences. For this reason it is essential for every rider to develop the habit of being able to step out distances and to know how the distance relates to the strides taken and, indeed, whether they are long or short strides. As a general rule, about 15½ paces (or yards) measure three non-jumping strides; 18 to 19 yards, four strides and 22 to 23 yards, five strides. Practise stepping out distances, and train yourself to cover 3ft with every step taken.

Riding the Course

Few course builders deliberately set out to trap a horse into making mistakes. At the same time if a course builder continually has over half the class going clear, he will soon be out of a job. Therefore he has to ask a few questions to test the ability of horse and rider. He will also be hoping that all the faults will not come at the same fence or two.

Faults obviously occur either from refusals or from poles being knocked down. It is interesting to reflect that the very obstacles which will stop a horse in his early life are the same ones that will keep him in the air when he becomes older and more experienced. Most natural jumpers begin by being very spooky about their fences. This is because they are naturally careful and do not like hitting poles: a very desirable trait. All but the very best tend to become more complacent as they grow older, and then the bolder the fence the less likely they are to hit it. The horse who as a raw novice takes fences on with little regard for his own safety (or that of his rider) rarely makes the grade over a long period.

In any novice competition the first two or three fences should be inviting and relatively trouble free. Unfortunately, this is not always the case in practice. Beware of the early fence which is solid and brightly painted – a sure-fire trap for the wary horse. Coloured hurdles and fillers are always harder to jump early in the course before a novice has had a chance to get well into his stride. Many young horses will have an odd stop at a wall. Be ready for it and keep them well up to the bridle from a strong leg pressure. A novice will usually back off a wall even under pressure and will generally make the effort to clear it. When jumping indoors, beware of related distances early in the course. Upon landing, most riders' natural reaction is to pick the horse up and hold him together in readiness for the next obstacle but, if the distance so dictates, sometimes the rider has to land and keep going. In this situation it is

Mercifully, not all courses are as big as this one, which was truly enormous for the third leg of the European Championships at Dinard in 1985. It decided the individual championship, which was ultimately won for a record-breaking third time by Paul Schockemöhle and the incredible Deister. Not surprisingly Nick Skelton and Michael Whitaker look happy enough. Only the day before they'd formed half of the team which took the gold medals by a massive five-fence margin. Dinard is one of the most popular venues on the international circuit and the organisers went out of their way to make the championships an unforgettable experience. They certainly succeeded in every way.

obviously an advantage to watch a few horses go in order to see exactly how the course and distances ride.

If a fence is inviting to jump, with a well-defined groundline, it should present little problem. With fences that have no groundline greater care is needed to place the horse correctly and to have him well collected and in the best possible outline to make a rounded jump. Fences which come into this category are most people's bogey fences: that is planks and stiles. With both of these fences it is essential really to have the horse together and not allow him to take the initiative himself by tackling them from a long flat stride and with far too much pace.

Spreads need a lot of analysing, too. The plain old-fashioned triple bar can be summed up in a few words: have enough pace and get to the bottom rail. If a horse stands off at a triple bar, he will be coming down when he should be going up and is likely to take the back rail with him. Parallel bars vary a great deal. The sloping type, with the back rail higher than the front, present few problems; but be sure to have enough movement to clear the back pole. Square oxers with both rails the same height take more jumping. This type of fence really needs riding more like a vertical because the front rail is the danger element. The rider should have the horse going well up into the hand, though not off a flat stride. Again, be sure to have enough impulsion to take care of the spread.

The most difficult parallel or oxer is the one with about four poles in one plane at the front, but with no groundline. By that I mean that the lowest pole is perhaps 1ft off the ground, the back pole is the same height as the top front rail and there is a brush fence in the middle. It is a square, difficult fence which is not easy for a horse to judge. It is even harder for a rider to get to correctly and arrive in the best spot to take off from a good approach and pace, whilst maintaining the best shape. The horse needs to be even more up into the bridle, with his hocks even more underneath him, and ultra light on the forehand. The front rail is the danger here – if you have to leave anything to chance, make it the back rail. Have a light but firm contact with the hands until the horse picks up to jump, and an even stronger than usual pressure from the lower leg literally to squeeze your horse up into the air and to make sure that he, in turn, makes more of an effort and concentrates on jumping the fence cleanly.

Consider the Going
The condition of surfaces in show jumping rings in Britain varies enormously, from bone-hard playing field-type

ground in high summer to the bog-like conditions sometimes encountered early in the season at farms owned by generous people who do not seem to mind having their fields torn apart by horses and lorries when the land has not had time to dry out after winter. All horses go better on good going. Out of doors, what is generally accepted as good is level pasture, or made-up ground in a stadium, with a dense covering of grass of a reasonable length. Ideally, the ground should be soft enough for a horse at the very least to leave a print of his hoof on the take-off and landing sides of fences. Indoors the opposite applies, and it is comparatively rare to get ground that is too firm. Usually the only problems arise when too much material on the surface makes the going too deep or when the surface chops up on the landing and take-off sides of fences.

There are very few shows on the circuit where one can be certain that the organisers will ensure the jumpers are given ideal conditions to produce their best form. But there are some major shows which consistently produce brilliant going. The Bath and West, held during the first week in June, is one. The Great Yorkshire, in July, is another. The major Hickstead meetings also have the benefit of irrigation facilities when required. Shows of that calibre are, of course, in the minority, and some thought needs to go into what can be done to improve conditions at local shows when the whole operation has to be run on a tight budget (and most of them do). I am sure that prevention is better than cure and that a lot of forward thinking is required to achieve good ground. The head groundsmen at Wimbledon and Wembley stadium start thinking about their playing surface more than a couple of weeks in advance of the tennis championships or cup final.

I do not think anyone would expect the smaller shows to be able to water their courses but certain things can be done to improve matters in the event of a long dry spell. The ground needs to be even underfoot. Hard ground is tough enough on horses' feet and joints but a rough, uneven surface is even more harmful. This means that the field needs to be well rolled in the spring while it is still soft enough to be worked. A good growth of grass is a great help. If the grass is becoming too long, running a grass topping machine over it at intervals will help enormously. The toppings, left behind as they fall, give the ground a bit of 'bottom'. There is no ground worse to jump on than that which has had hay or silage taken off it a week or two before.

LIBRARY
BISHOP BURTON COLLEGE
BEVERLEY HU17 8QG

When watering is out of the question the next best thing is spreading sand on the take-off and landing sides of fences. Admittedly this might also stretch the finances of the smaller shows, but even an odd load or two dropped at the practice fence is money well spent. Most horses jump as many fences outside the ring as they do inside, and being prepared on soft landings will at least get them into the ring in the right frame of mind. Let us not forget the most important thing of all: it is always the good horse who suffers most from bad going. Because he is seldom out of the jump-off he nearly always has to go twice and of course has also to be warmed up at the practice fence twice. Good horses are not easy to come by and it is amazing how many of the decent ones I have had through my hands were just not the soundest. Perhaps one notices it more with good horses. Because one tends to look after them, they last for years, whereas the less talented individual (who never seems to have a day's lameness in his life) is usually transfer-listed somewhere along the line.

Having got all that about bad ground off my chest, perhaps a thought or two as to how to handle it would not be out of place. As with a car, there is only so much mileage in each horse. There are only so many times in his life that he can land over a fence and hit the ground before some wear and tear becomes apparent. The longer you can avert that situation the better. Harvey Smith once said to me that if a horse is sound, the older he gets the better he gets. If he is unsound, the older he gets the worse he gets. I am sure he is right. Horses who are feeling the effects of hard ground concentrate more on the pain they experience when landing than on jumping the fences. Their stride shortens and they rapidly begin to associate pain and discomfort with jumping fences. That is a frame of mind to be avoided at all costs. I would far rather leave one or two horses in the lorry than pull them out and jump on diabolical ground. Even if I won a class that day, it might cost me several others in subsequent weeks. To look at it another way, saving a horse while the ground is bad will inevitably pay dividends when the rain comes, for the simple reason that you will have a sound horse, well in his mind and ready to do his job efficiently, when most of the others around him will be defending themselves because of their recent unpleasant experiences.

What Type of Studs?
As a general rule some form of studs to prevent horses from slipping are essential equipment. Certainly horses can jump without them, but they will be a lot more

confident on their feet with a bit more traction, especially against the clock. However, it is a hassle to keep stud holes clean and usable. They rapidly fill up with earth and grit and have to be laboriously picked out at every show before the studs are put in. I tend either to fill them with cotton wool between classes or to fit very shallow, square sleepers, which not only serve to keep the holes clean and usable but also act as good studs for roadwork. On show days, after having had a good look at the going, I go back to the lorry and tell the girls what type of studs to put in which horse and how many. Over recent seasons I have changed from one stud for each hoof to two, one in each heel. I feel that this balances a horse's foot more and, obviously, it doubles the grip, which is tremendously beneficial, especially when going against the clock.

How Often to Compete

There is no hard and fast rule as to how often a horse can compete. Some horses, like some humans, can stand more work than others, but with a good horse, even if he can stand a lot of work, it does not follow that you can keep pulling him out class after class. The two things which are important to consider are the horse's physical and mental

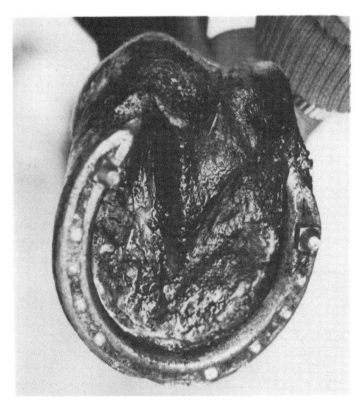

On firm ground I'd sometimes not use studs at all in the front feet. If I did, I'd pick out the smallest and sharpest ones in the box, so as to reduce the jar on a horse's foot as much as possible. The sharp studs pictured here are some of the smallest, coming almost to a point, and having just enough square shoulder on them to accommodate the spanner. I sometimes use these in the front feet combined with the back feet studs shown in the bottom photograph on page 156.

Small, square, block studs, ideal for use when there's a bit of give in the ground. Block studs come in various sizes and can be used without any problem as long as you're sure that they can get into the ground. I'd use studs like these in front, combined with studs behind such as those in the photograph below.

An ideal wet-weather stud. These large studs are really good when there's a lot of give in the ground in wet conditions. They are big blocks really, but have the edges rounded off so that they go into the ground more easily. They're ideal studs for use in the hind feet, and with these you can ask for some pretty tight turns against the clock and be reasonably confident of not slipping all over the place.

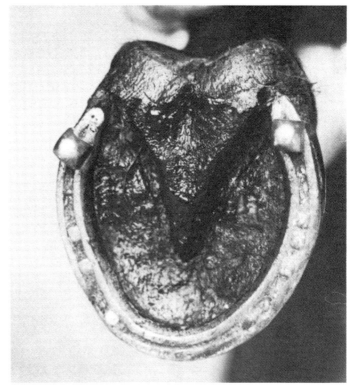

welfare – with wear and tear very much uppermost in the mind – and just how often a horse needs to jump to produce his best form. Some horses jump better fresh and, like some racehorses, can come out and win first time. Others need a class or two to get their eye in and then, if competed with at intervals which suit their mentality and physical make-up, should consistently produce their best form.

Various factors influence how often a horse jumps: for example, if I go to a three-day show, I will more often than not only jump each horse in one class a day. But if I go to a weekend show with novice horses, who probably will not jump again until the following weekend, I will quite happily jump two classes a day, as long as the going is not bad. However, I do try wherever possible to reward a horse who has jumped two clears and been near the top end of the line in one class by leaving it at that for the day.

It is expecting too much of a weekend rider who has limited opportunity for competition, and who goes to great trouble and expense to go to a show at all, to pull out for only one class – especially if he has only one horse. As long as a horse is not asked to do it several days running, it is not unreasonable to ask him to jump two classes in one day. At least for the second class he will not need much working-in or many jumps at the practice fence. Commonsense must prevail. A good horse who gives you everything he has got every time out, who tries to jump fences cleanly all the time and will almost literally bust a gut to win a class for you, naturally deserves far more consideration than a bone-headed hooligan whose waking hours are consistently spent making life difficult for his rider. Unfortunately, given a straight choice between the two, in most outfits it would be the former who would get the most jumping rather than the latter.

It is a point worth remembering that at shows such as Wembley, Olympia or Hickstead, which are of four or more days' duration, top riders will almost invariably give their best horse a day off before the Grand Prix. They see the wisdom of resting a horse, and are, virtually without exception, rewarded with a better performance in the class that really matters. It is not difficult to employ those tactics at all levels.

CHAPTER 9

Getting to Know the Business

Doubles and Trebles

The majority of mistakes in a round are made at the double or treble. From a satisfactory approach horses certainly make fewer faults at single fences, for the simple reason that there is only one element to think about. Combination fences are a different matter and each needs to be examined individually as to its construction, siting, height and width. Even the most novice of riders can easily appreciate that, for example, a big and long double of parallel bars uphill and away from home is going to need a lot of power, and is sure to catch a lot of horses.

However, there are many other factors to be taken into consideration with combinations, since there are so many variations on the theme. Horses will never make distance in a combination fence, or jump out well, if they do not make a good jump in. You must train them to do so. Many young horses develop hang-ups about doubles and trebles – and I mean that quite literally, because the spooky horse who loses impulsion, and consequently distance, will always have trouble making the back rail of a spread in a double. As a result he becomes even more frightened, loses more distance and eventually pulls up altogether. Horses must always be taught to jump into a double boldly but with care.

I suppose I subconsciously build combinations at home a fair size smaller than those one would normally meet in the ring. As a general rule I feel that this can work to a horse's advantage. Although with single fences I occasionally hang up a big vertical or pull a spread out a foot or two, I try to avoid making horses struggle in combinations at home at any stage of their career. It is better to foster the belief that the horse can jump anything he is asked to without doubting himself or his rider.

It is essential for a rider, however inexperienced, to learn as quickly as possible how to step out distances and to know whether they are short, normal or long. Almost without exception, experienced riders can step out distances in combinations and tell you to the nearest inch or two how they will ride. Granted, you will learn a lot simply from watching a few horses go, but if you are in the first three in the order, you really must have an accurate idea at what pace to ride into any combination. It is best to train yourself to take a stride of 3ft when stepping out a distance. Practise at home. Step out your own distances in combinations and ride through them. Sometimes make them longer, sometimes shorter (within reason). Keep the fences quite low, ride the distance again, and really get a feel for it.

When competing, look out for those places on the course where most faults are occurring. Ask yourself why and how to ride that one, so that the same does not happen to you. Simple things, such as whether a double is jumped away from the entrance or towards it, make a lot of difference to some horses.

Learn to study combination fences and ask yourself which element, if any, is going to be the troublesome one. A big vertical fence into a double or treble always takes a lot of jumping and will stop a horse dead in his tracks if he hits it hard enough. Always approach this sort of fence from a short, powerful stride, with the horse going into the bridle from a strongly supportive leg. To get in well he has to make a really good jump in front; but if the distance is quite long, he also has to go in with plenty of power in order to come out the other end. Pace alone is not sufficient because sheer pace usually goes hand in hand with a long, flat stride and he will almost certainly mow down the vertical going in. A parallel going into a double is usually easier. The horse can come in off a normal stride, and the fence itself encourages him to make a better jump. Again, the rider's leg needs to support the horse, to anticipate any backward thinking and to ensure that there is impulsion enough to get out at the other end. Remember that in the interests of producing confident jumpers as well as of self-preservation it is always preferable to hit a fence in front rather than to become hung up on a back rail behind.

As another example, take a treble of vertical, long stride to parallel and long stride to triple bar, both very wide spreads. If the horse has scope and takes the treble with plenty of pace, he should jump through without a problem. But what happens if the first distance is a yard shorter? No chance of blazing down into that one at a gallop. That way, the horse would have little chance of jumping the front rail of the parallel, and because his pace would carry him in further, he would shorten the distance even more, back off the front rail to jump it, land short over the parallel and have little chance of making the distance to the triple bar. The skilful rider with an obedient horse would be more likely to come from a steady, more collected approach, take care to jump the vertical and land short over it, and only then really move to jump the parallel and triple bar.

That is only one of the many problems with which the course builder is likely to test horses. It follows that the type of horse required needs to have scope, to be careful and brave at the same time, and to be schooled to the highest level.

Related Distances

When the distance between two fences is more than can normally be taken in two strides, it is a related distance. If there are more than five strides between fences, there is usually space enough for a bit of reorganisation from the saddle. However, over big courses it is often useful to step out distances up to seven strides (about 31 yards). With big fences, it is important for a rider to know whether he must ride hard from the previous fence – to jump, for example, a long and strong combination – or to hold the horse up on a short stride to jump a big vertical downhill. The latter often happens at Hickstead, where the gradient plays a big part in the technique needed to jump various parts of every course.

Although distances between fences are the same for everyone, horses' strides vary enormously. For this reason it is essential to be accurate when stepping out a distance. A horse normally covers around 12ft (four human steps) to one non-jumping stride. A three-stride distance is about 15 to 16 yards; four strides, about 19 yards or a little over; five strides, around 23 yards, and six, 27 to 28 yards.

As a general rule I always encourage novice horses and riders to go on the distance which the course builder intended. With schooling, a horse can be trained to take out a stride to save time when really going against the clock, or to put in an extra stride for a more precise approach. But basically, if a distance walks, for example, four strides, then ride to the first part with every intention of taking four. That way both horse and rider know where they stand.

When jumping indoors it is even more important to understand related distances, because there is less space and therefore less margin for error. Also, most distances indoors are built on straight lines. Outdoor distances can sometimes be built with a second fence at an angle to the first, which I think is intelligent course designing – fences set in that way allow a rider to use the radius of the bend to his advantage to put in an extra stride and keep the horse in a better shape to jump. If you have sufficient fences at home, a line of anything from three to six fences is a good education. When you turn a corner to a long line of fences it is an imposing sight and immediately commands a horse's whole attention, as well as testing the rider to the full if they are all set at precise related distances. When building such a line, keep the fences reasonably low and walk it on foot first, to give yourself an accurate idea as to exactly how you are going to ride it.

Half Strides

It is one thing to know whether or not a distance is going to ride a true level stride but something else entirely to know what to do about it if it is not. Obviously a lot depends on the horse, his ability and his length of stride. Where a distance has definitely, and quite justifiably, been set up by a course designer to test the rider's skill, the rider must have a clearly defined plan as to how to ride that distance to suit his own horse. The majority of horses are best served by putting in an extra stride rather than taking one out. It is always better to keep a horse up together on a short, round stride rather than opening him up and getting him flat on a long one. For example, a 21-yard distance would in most cases be best jumped from five strides rather than four, at least at novice level. An older horse could come on a longer stride and pick up the distance easily enough to make it in four without any ill effects. But it is always a bad thing to train a novice to run at fences off long, flat strides.

A lot depends on the nature of the fence. If the first part of a related distance is a wide spread followed off a short distance by a big vertical (the most popular course designer's trap), then there can only really be one way to ride it: pick up the horse as soon as he lands over the spread and hold him together all the way to the vertical, keeping him light on the forehand, with his hocks well under him and in a good outline to jump the vertical. From a vertical to a big spread would, of course, be entirely the opposite. First make sure of jumping the vertical, but on landing keep moving to the next fence and without flapping or letting the horse become flat, make up the distance and maintain enough impulsion not only to jump the first rail but also to get across the back rail of the spread.

Again, it is so important to be able to walk the distance and know exactly how you are going to ride it. Even then it is all too easy to change your mind or be influenced by how other horses cope with it. Horses' strides vary enormously and no one can know more about a horse's stride than his own rider. I clearly remember an example of that one night at Wembley a few years ago. Fence 2 was a big square parallel off the corner, followed in a straight line by 5ft 3ins planks at what, as far as I can remember, was 18 yards, which was unusual to say the least, especially so early in the course. When walking the course there was the usual consternation and head scratching from groups of riders who had to make decisions as to how to ride it on their own individual horses. I had finally decided to go on three, as Sunorra was always best suited to bowling along rather than being held up off short strides. Being early to go – about third or fourth – I did not have much opportunity to watch other horses tackle the distance. But, still a little doubtful, I had a practice jump early and ran in to watch the first one go. It was Harvey Smith, who jumped it easily enough off four strides. I made the fatal mistake of going against my better judgement and, changing my mind, decided to go for four. In fact the four strides really were not there for my horse and she hit the planks in front. It was stupid, for I am sure she could have got there easily enough from three. But there's nothing like hindsight, is there?

Courses and Course Builders
The British Show Jumping Association lays down such extensive guidelines to govern the construction of courses that in theory there should be little difference between one and another. But the way in which a course designer interprets those guidelines, and the material he has at his disposal to build with, can vary so much that a course may be right up one horse's street but a near impossibility for another. At whatever level you compete, whether it be riding club, unaffiliated, or right up to international level, the course designer is a tremendously important person. Rather like horses, course builders' ability and temperament can vary widely.

It is only fair, too, to point out that it is a very poorly paid job; the majority of people at local level count themselves lucky even to receive food and expenses. It is difficult, sometimes tedious, work, often in the coldest and wettest weather, and bear in mind, too, that most people find it far easier to criticse than to praise. But, having said all that, from the rider's point of view he has every right to be critical – provided he knows what he is talking about – because the courses which young horses jump influence

them for the rest of their careers.

I try to avoid the course designer who does not know what he is doing and makes blatant errors (nearly always with distances) because he knows no better. I far prefer to ride the courses of someone who has competed himself, has a feel for what horses can reasonably be expected to jump and has their best interests at heart. It is always a pleasure to ride round the novice courses of designers who also build at top level, especially if they are former riders themselves. Pam Carruthers, Jon Doney and Bob Ellis all come into this category and I would always be influenced to go to a show where one of their names was on the schedule.

Pam Carruthers was the senior course designer at Hickstead for more than twenty-five years, and was also in big demand worldwide. She spends a great deal of her time abroad: in fact most of the winter in New Zealand. She is in no small part responsible for the improvement of the sport in that part of the world. Although she will continue as technical delegate at Hickstead, she retired as course designer in 1987 and handed over to Jon Doney who has had a lifetime's involvement with the sport. His course designing skill and integrity make him, too, in very big

Course builder Jon Doney, who has had a lifetime's experience with horses.

163

demand. An important figure in BSJA administration, he is to be seen at many shows, large and small, throughout the country, ensuring that the machinery is working properly at all levels. The sport could do with more like him.

Apart from assisting with the courses at such shows as Wembley and Olympia, Bob Ellis is in great demand at local level because, having competed extensively himself, he has a natural feel for what is right for a young horse. His courses are sympathetic, pleasurable to ride, and seem to reward the better horses, which is as it should be. Never one to get masses of clear rounds, Bob is among that rare breed of course builders who is infinitely aware of how many young horses can be ruined by mind-blowing galloping against the clock as novices.

The majority of riders, myself included, are a very critical group of individuals when it comes to what their horses are asked to jump. Who can blame them? Good horses are very difficult to come by and, if asked unreasonable questions too often, will have their competitive lives shortened accordingly.

Obviously, what suits one type of horse will not suit another, and no one expects to have things entirely their own way all the time. But what most riders would like to see are courses which will not only provide entertainment for the paying public and television viewers, but will also enable horses to compete for many seasons, winning in their turn and, most important, retaining their enthusiasm for the job.

The standard of competition today requires that courses need to be demanding enough. But that does not mean that they should be built without a sympathetic feel and an understanding of what riders believe are reasonable questions to ask their horses. Results can be achieved without horses being taken to the limit nearly every time they go into the ring.

Nobody minds big verticals – a high fence looks impressive to the public and does not demoralise a horse. Similarly, a big square parallel is a very fair test and, if well sited, will raise few complaints from competitors. On the other hand, a long combination with sloping parallels only serves to get horses stretched to the utmost and obtains results not by testing pure jumping ability (surely what the game is all about), but by brute force and power, with little finesse attached to it.

All the above comments mainly relate to the British competitive scene, but of course top riders also have to compete abroad against the best in the world. One often hears it said that a certain horse would be a very good winner in England, meaning that he is a careful jumper and respects his fences. Courses abroad tend to be built with heavier poles and longer distances, so it would be shortsighted from an international point of view to allow our best horses to compete solely over light poles, narrow spreads and short combinations.

Hickstead is a good testing ground for international horses. There the courses have a truly European flavour, and are built with one of the best sets of fences in the world, surely a course builder's dream.

Against the Clock

I believe that horses jumping at top level and at county shows have just about reached their limits as far as height and width are concerned. Classes are being won and lost by the smallest possible margins, even down to one-hundredth of a second, which is an incredibly fine dividing line. That major competitions should be divided in this way is inevitable; so too are the more demanding courses and distance problems required to divide the abundance of high class riders and horses that we are fortunate enough to have in Britain.

What is less pleasant, at least to my mind, is that novice and local competitions seem to become correspondingly faster. That situation cannot be beneficial to anyone, least of all to the horse whom we are trying to educate to be our star of tomorrow. Granted the young horse has to be taught to turn sharply, to attack a big fence from a short approach, to jump a fence on an angle and even to take the odd one or two from the gallop, but this does not mean that he should have to pull out all the stops every time he is in a jump-off.

It is for this reason that I feel you should plan exactly how fast you feel your particular young horse should be asked to go, assuming that you really have his best interests at heart and are not out to win every class at all costs. Of course, every horse is different. Some horses are stuffy animals who do not become over-excited under pressure and would on occasions even benefit from being driven to the limit. This, however, is the exception. What you have to consider is the nice young horse, who has a big heart and an honest mind and jump, which you would like to preserve – the sort of animal who, although he is genuine and an honest trier, would perhaps become disenchanted with show jumping if he had his mind blown every time he reached a jump-off.

At the end of the first round in any competition it is

usually relatively easy to predict whether a jump-off is going to be a 'flier', or whether a second clear round in a reasonable time would see you well up in the money. To put it another way, it is 'make-up-your-mind-time'. Either you are going to have a real cut or you are not. In many cases there are grounds for taking a good young horse more slowly than is needed to win a particular class, especially if the rider has it in mind to win bigger and better competitions with his horse at a later date. There is a lot of satisfaction to be gained from jumping a nice educational round and finishing in the lower placings. The horse will have learned a bit more about his job and the rider will feel that he has made his contribution to that learning process. However, I do not think it does a horse any harm to learn to turn short to a fence when he is a novice; that is all part of his education, as is jumping the odd fence at a slight angle. He must learn about the different line that has to be taken when going against the clock in preparation for the day when his rider says go and really means it.

One factor which influences the result of any jump-off against the clock is the draw. Obviously, if a horse is drawn last or nearly last, it makes the rider's job much simpler because he knows exactly what he has to do to win, though for a novice rider this may be a handicap because he is then under more pressure. If you are drawn very early, things are not quite so simple. It is then a question of weighing up the opposition. How many are there to follow you? Do the course and the turns suit your horse? Most horses jump better off one rein than the other, and if all the crunch turns are on his bad rein, this definitely will not help. If the rider can learn to anticipate roughly how many of his opponents are going to go clear again in the jump-off, it will help him to plan just how fast a standard he needs to set. Of course, if the class is obviously going to be flat out, he just has to set sail and take as many chances as possible – though not so many that he would be highly unlikely to go clear.

Before setting off it is not a bad plan to ride over to any really difficult turn on the course and to have a quick, close look at it before the bell goes to send you on your way. It helps to have in mind a chosen line. That line should be as tight as you dare turn on that particular horse without standing him on his head. If a difficult turn is back to a vertical, you can take a very big chance, as the worst that can happen is that the horse will hit it in front or will stop. If there is a turn back to a big parallel or a combination involving spread fences, take much more care. A horse is more likely to make a fault there, and if a turn is over-

I very rarely ask horses to go fast at home. Nevertheless it's beneficial to the young horse to learn, from quite an early age, to turn tightly to fences and to jump at a slight angle. Here I'm preparing to turn quite short to the next fence. The mare is unaware that she's about to turn because I've next to no weight on the rein, otherwise I'd be in danger of making her cramp her hind legs and take a brick with her. I already have my body weight going where I want to be. The inside (left) hand is poised ready to look after the direction, while the outside hand and leg will stop the horse from drifting on the corner.

cooked, he may receive a bad fright as well.

When setting off, have your horse going well up into the bridle. Let him stride along a little and have a sense of urgency about him, but without getting him worried and out of his rhythm. If the first fence is very easy and can be disregarded as a danger fence, it is possible to save a second or so from the time you go through the timing heads to when you land over the first. Since every horse is different, pick out where to take chances and where to be cautious. If your worst fence (probably everyone else's too) is late in the course, a lot of time has to be saved early on to allow for an extra check or a wider turn into the danger fence. If, on the other hand a difficult fence is early on, it often pays to get the major problem out of the way and then go for home as hard as possible.

Remember that if a horse is turned sharply into a big fence, he is just as likely to jump it as if he were given a long approach, because the turn and size of the fence will surprise him into making more effort. But this will only work in your favour if the horse has been accurately turned from a well-balanced approach. Finally, do not forget the final chance to save a split second from the last fence to the finish line. Remember, it is split seconds which win classes.

Time Faults

The clock plays an ever bigger part in modern show jumping. While I cannot agree with the speed at which young horses are asked to go to be anywhere near winning their competitions, I am equally certain that, at least from an entertainment viewpoint, the clock will continue to play a big part in the future. The majority of competitions for young horses are run at 300 or 320 metres per minute, while a Nations Cup and some other major competitions are run at 400 metres. It is a considerable step up in speed, and riders simply cannot hang about or they will certainly get time faults.

I can be as guilty as anyone else of picking up the odd time fault, so I am hardly in a position to criticise. But I do think that it is no bad plan to teach a horse quite early in his career to go the shortest way. This allows the rider to spend that all important little bit more time in getting from one fence to another in the best possible manner. Get into the habit of checking the time allowed before a competition. Look at the course plan. If it is a BSJA affiliated show, a course plan must be posted adjacent to the collecting ring, and the time allowed will be shown on it. If there are a few horses in the class before you, watch two or

Experienced horses can be asked to turn in the air or jump at an angle. This photograph was taken in South Africa. My borrowed horse is really trying, as can be seen by the way he's tucking his legs away. I'm preparing to take a sharp left inside the parallel to jump the fence in the top left of the picture. It's obvious from my position which way I'm preparing to go on landing. On the other hand, he appears ready to go straight ahead. The fence he's jumping is the last of a treble and he's wisely getting that out of the way before thinking any further. Incidentally, this horse habitually jumped to the left and is dangerously close to the wing here. In fairness, he never made a mistake through this habit, although it was sometimes a little nerveracking in doubles and trebles.

three go and just take a rough time check on a wristwatch which has a second hand. Top riders do that automatically with the first one or two in any competition, checking their finishing times on the digital display clock and comparing them with the time allowed. Courses are often measured wrongly and some courses builders are reluctant to admit that they have made a mistake and to alter the time accordingly – which the rules permit them to do when the first three to five horses have jumped.

Watch the Professionals

There is a great deal to be learned by quite simply standing and watching successful riders. It is no fluke that they have reached the top. Show jumping is a tough, hard business and – leaving aside the odd rider who briefly makes it to the top – novices can learn much by observing the methods of those riders who compete on many horses, year in, year out, at the highest level. A horse's basic schooling and preparation for a competition is to a great extent responsible for his success because however good he is a horse will win few classes if badly prepared and ridden. Someone once remarked to me that members of the public are given a free show jumping lesson every time they stand at the collecting ring of a major show. I am sure he was right: there is a great deal more to be learned watching a good rider set up his horse outside than there is to be gained watching the finished article go in there and win.

Riders' styles vary considerably but when you really get down to it there is very little difference in the way they prepare and ride their horses. The same basic principles apply to all. The use of the leg and hand; the shape and outline they look for; the muscle development and condition of their horses; the way they all insist on agreeable obedience in their flat work; the supple way in which a horse bends and carries himself, and a balanced, rhythmic pace, are virtually common to all. Of course, the amount of preparation varies from horse to horse. Some may need a lot of working in, either because they are cold-blooded animals who need to get the adrenalin running, or hot ones who need to have some gas letting off.

The amount of practice jumps a horse requires also varies a lot. I am often asked how much jumping a horse should be given before he goes into a class but, as with so many other things, there are no hard and fast rules. However, to spend an hour or so beside the practice ring before a big competition will tell the novice rider the answers to many questions if he is prepared to be patient and observant. Try to analyse the relationship between a rider's preparation and the finished article in the arena: why a certain horse goes in the way he does and how this is influenced by the work he has done beforehand. Notice in particular the degree of collection and control a rider asks for and try to relate that to how he goes in the ring when the rider opens his hand a little and moves the horse forward to the fences. There is so much to be learned just by looking and listening.

Upgrading

There is an old saying: 'Keep yourself in the best company and your horses in the worst.' Though I do not think it is 100 per cent true for show jumping, there is a fair amount of sense in it. Many people become confused as to just which class to jump their horses in because there is such a variety of competitions on offer in present-day schedules. My answer to the question, 'When should I take a step up in class?' is that a horse will tell you when he is ready, simply by jumping his share of double clear rounds. Some horses are natural winners and run up through the grades very quickly, whereas others, although they, too, jump their share of clear rounds, rarely seem actually to win a class – and so take longer to upgrade.

Except with truly outstanding horses, I do not believe in jumping them a long way out of their grade, for example putting Newcomers horses in Grade C classes or Foxhunter horses in quite strong opens. A good horse will get there soon enough, and his way of going and consistency will be all the information a rider needs to know when to move up a grade. The worst person in the world to kid is yourself. You have to be very realistic about a horse's capabilities. Over-ambition can be costly and has ruined many young horses, who have been over-faced with bigger courses than they or their riders have been capable of jumping at that stage in their careers. You do not need anyone to send you a postcard when you have a really good horse, because his ability will be there for all to see and should be matched by a consistent record.

A student will often ask me what I really think about his or her horse, and the odd one may be really put out if I say that, in my opinion, the horse is not good enough and is a waste of time. The business is really too expensive to persevere for very long with a horse who is not going to improve. Of course, there are exceptions to every rule, and a good many decent campaigners produce consistent results year in, year out at their own level and do nobody any harm. But a horse who has no real ability, and probably the wrong temperament as well, will rarely provide anyone with enjoyment and is best transfer-listed.

It is impossible to say at just what level a rider should aim. Different people want different things from the game. The person who competes at club level and never aspires to anything greater can derive every bit as much enjoyment from show jumping as the person who gets the breaks, and the right horses and has the ability and backing to go a lot further. The vast majority of riders are in the business purely for enjoyment. It is surely better to jump at a level where you can be competitive and have a chance to win in your turn than to aim too high, over-face the horse, and ultimately become disillusioned. Somewhere along the line it is probably advisable for a novice rider to seek advice from a professional trainer and to act upon that advice. No reputable trainer would knowingly give a rider unreliable information, but would far rather impart sound advice based on long experience of the sport.

CHAPTER 10

The BSJA

Every show jumping nation in the world has its own official governing body which is in turn affiliated to the FEI (Fédération Equestre Internationale). At the time of writing, some 86 countries were affiliated to the FEI, and the numbers increase year by year. There is no doubt that show jumping is a growth sport and a very international one, too.

Britain's national federation, the British Show Jumping Association, was founded in 1923 and operates from an office building which it shares jointly with the British Horse Society on the Royal Showground at Stoneleigh in Warwickshire. The day-to-day administration is the responsibility of the Secretary-General and his team. Major decisions are handled by the executive committee which meets in London four or five times a year. This committee, around eighteen strong, is made up of eight nationally and ten regionally elected members. In addition, two members are nominated by the Scottish branch. Half the elected members retire each year and are eligible to stand for re-election, and the committee elects its own Chairman annually. The executive committee receives reports from various subordinate standing committees, such as finance, international affairs, training and rules.

The Association publishes the BSJA Rules and Yearbook annually and its own newspaper, *The BSJA News*, four times a year. These publications go to members free of charge, and the Association also publishes a monthly show bulletin, available by subscription, giving brief details of a comprehensive list of affiliated shows throughout the year.

As in any other sport, the governing body comes in for some criticism, and the BSJA is no exception, but I am sure of one thing – they have the interests of the show jumping world uppermost in their minds and committee decisions are not lightly made by people who really care for the sport.

The BSJA is ever conscious of forging the link between unaffiliated competitors and those who feel ready to join

The driving force behind the PR department of the British Show Jumping Association is the Press Officer, Liz Dudden, who has the respect of everyone for her hard work and efficiency. A former journalist, Liz holds the reins of a very important post in the organisation and does it extremely well. She is also blessed with a great sense of humour, which makes a difficult job more fun both for her and for the people she has to deal with.

International Affairs Secretary Jacky Wood has the onerous task of organising senior teams representing Britain abroad. She's present at all international affairs and selection meetings and has to organise travelling, hotels, stables, entries and numerous other items to smooth the path for riders, owners and horses. She's worked for the BSJA for virtually all of her career and would be very difficult to replace.

the Association. Great steps have been made over the last year or two to encourage new membership at grass roots level. The present structure of novice show jumping is heavily geared to making it worthwhile for club-level riders to affiliate.

To Affiliate or Not

As mentioned in the previous chapter, a horse will tell you when he is ready for a step-up in class by jumping plenty of clear rounds at his present level. Any horse who is regularly competing at unaffiliated shows will easily cope with the new BSJA novice competitions run at similar heights. In fact, some unaffiliated shows have courses considerably bigger than their official counterparts – in some cases over inferior fences and without the benefit of a qualified course builder. There must surely be a lot more satisfaction to be had from jumping in official shows. It gives a rider a great kick to win the first few pounds in affiliated competitions and to have it entered in his official computer record, which is readily available from the Association's offices.

Novice riders can learn a great deal by sharing the collecting ring with one or two local international stars, who will inevitably be schooling their own novice horses at local shows between competing on their Grade A horses. It is traditionally every rider's dream to qualify for the Horse of the Year Show at Wembley in October. National competitors now have one complete day set aside for them at this show, as well as other competitions during the week, so the incentive is better than ever.

It is not expensive to join the Association and because the BSJA is all out to win over the young and non-affiliated riders, it has made membership as attractive as possible. The novice rider is unlikely to progress very far at unaffiliated shows, since he has little of value, either riders or horses, with which to compare himself – simply because most good riders will already have graduated to bigger things. There can be little harm in having a go at affiliated shows, and nowadays, with the present novice-class structure, riders can even compete free of charge and then opt to pay a subscription if they qualify for a championship and if they decide to continue to compete at affiliated level. A good introduction to affiliated jumping could be the smallest class at a local country show, perhaps organised by the hunt – they are always very sound affairs. Most such shows have a second ring where the fences and competition are just that bit easier than in the main ring. Many shows these days put on a clear-round class to start the day, so it is often possible to have a rehearsal before the first main class and to give the horse an opportunity to jump round the course.

I cannot help feeling what a brilliant class the Pathfinders competition is: horses only jump two rounds, and the jump-off is not against the clock, all double clear rounds dividing first. One ever-present bee in my bonnet is the number of good young horses who must be ruined by idiotic galloping against the clock when the poor animals hardly know how to jump. How often in novice competitions do you see twenty or thirty (or more) clears going flat out, learning only to jump low and flat? Under such circumstances they forget how their riders have mostly tried, quite rightly, to train them to work on the flat in a good shape at a nice even pace, with their minds in full control of their actions.

A few years ago the BSJA recommended that show organisers put on more competitions run under Table A1, all horses dividing first after three rounds, the final round not against the clock. It was felt, quite correctly in my view, that more good young horses would be produced that way. That the vast majority of shows did not pick up on it is a great pity. It goes without saying that the general public likes to see a timed jump-off, but the majority of novice classes do not play to packed houses anyway.

I think that the Irish have got it right. Virtually all their novice classes are divided after the first jump-off. This has many advantages. The horses are not over-jumped and are better able to cope with their job. Since Ireland is a country largely devoted to producing and selling horses, it is helpful if a horse's record shows that he has divided first in several competitions rather than had a few minor placings down the line and perhaps only the odd outright win. The riders are merely competing against the course, not each other, which surely makes it easier to jump a nice educational round.

Another little point which is not generally known over here is that horses in Ireland are allowed into the ring before the class, to inspect the fences, as used to be the case in England many years ago. I am not suggesting that we revert to this practice, but with a very green horse it cannot do any harm.

Grading by Money

Every country seems to have its own method of grading horses (and ponies). I am not convinced that Britain's is the right one, but it has certainly improved in recent years, the grading thresholds having been raised considerably. At one time it was possible for a young horse to win through to Grade A in little more than a season, even less in some cases. For example, when Flying Wild won her Foxhunter final in 1968 she was five years old; she had never jumped a fence in competition before Easter and was Grade A by August. Granted, she was a pretty exceptional novice, but many others have gone a similar way. It is one thing to start as a novice and win through the grades in one season with the benefit of continuity, but quite another to have six months' break and to try to pick up the following year, with a six-year-old, where you left off. Most young horses who have shot to the top too quickly take a temporary backward step at some time, usually in their second season. Flying Wild certainly did. Although she subsequently competed at top level for many years, she won no more in her second season than she did in her first.

Now that Grade A competitions are for horses having won £1000 and over, the situation is much better because very few horses could win that amount from scratch in their first year, when the majority of prizes they compete for as real novices would be around the £8 to £12 mark. Since Grade B is for horses having won £450 or more, it gives a long educational period to the Grade C horses having won under that figure. Even £450 takes a bit of winning with an average novice and up to that figure there really are a multitude of minor championships to be qualified for, thus giving everyone a shot at one or two nice competitions. For example the Grade C horse is very well catered for at Wembley, and in fact several horses at the 1986 show had qualified for all three major novice championships.

The Foxhunter series of competitions, which has its final at Wembley, is not quite as easy as it once was, having risen a fair bit over the years above its original status as the first rung of the ladder for novices. With the present dimensions of Foxhunter courses, which can be up to 3ft 11in in preliminary rounds and must include a double and a treble (in fact the height can rise to 4ft 5in in the highly competitive regional finals) you need a fairly decent horse to jump them.

The Newcomers competition does a good job for the new entry, with its upper limit of £80 winnings. The course cannot exceed 3ft 7in in the preliminary competitions (4ft 1in in the final) and it, too, has its final at Wembley for horses who have won through their regional finals.

The BSJA appears really to have hit the jackpot with the new British Novice Championship preliminary rounds, started in 1986 under the sponsorship of Badminton Horse Feeds. As I said in the previous chapter, this is a competition which is geared to linking the unaffiliated horse world to the Association. Horses cannot have won more than £20 in affiliated show jumping competitions and the preliminary rounds are open to both members and non-members of the Association. The course, restricted as it is to 2ft 9in in height or spread in these preliminary competitions, is suitable for the most inexperienced horses of all and serves its purposes if used, as was intended, as an educational stepping stone. Unfortunately, because the course is so lenient, most of these classes quite simply turn into a race, which really defeats the object. But the man has not yet been born who could devise a rule book to please everyone and to cover every eventuality.

Qualification (Getting a Quart into a Pint Pot)
Have you ever been disappointed at not seeing one of your favourite riders at such shows as Wembley, the Royal International or Olympia? The chances are that it was not that rider's choice to be elsewhere but simply because he or she had not qualified in that particular year. Obviously the big shows can accommodate only a certain number of entries and, because so many horses and riders are both good enough to be there and want to be, it has become essential to operate a separate qualifying system, designed to be as fair as possible to everyone, for each of those events. Any system of qualification invariably leads to some form of criticism from someone. What suits one does not suit another. But overall I think it is roundabouts and swings, and in most cases if the horse and rider are good enough they will get there anyway.

Of course, not so very long ago the Horse of the Year Show at Wembley marked the end of the show jumping season. Horses were roughed off within days of getting home, disappearing into winter quarters and oblivion until the following Easter. Not so nowadays. Various changes within the system and the structure of shows have ensured that every rider who wants to stay ahead of the game must keep his nose to the grindstone all the year round. At the top end there is simply no way that the part-time rider and complete amateur can keep up with everyone else. If a rider does not travel virtually every month of the year in order to win enough money – which, converted into points, keeps riders at the top end of the computer list – he quite simply does not get into the bigger shows mentioned above. Apart from the publicity and television coverage so dear to sponsors, it is those shows which carry the largest prize money and in turn help those same riders to re-qualify for subsequent big shows. To a great extent, Olympia started a new trend. We have all jumped indoors now for many years, but mainly at novice level – top riders have little time in the summer to bring on novices. The pre-Christmas Olympia spectacular has given international riders a new focal point to the year. Because of the show's immense popularity with riders (as well as its enviable box office appeal), many people now plan their whole winter programme to revolve around Olympia – taking in, of course, other European shows between Wembley and the finals of the World Cup in the early spring.

The World Cup series provides a tremendous winter boost for show jumping and appears to be here to stay. The sheer quality of the jumping in the final, held every second year at Gothenburg in Sweden and in other countries in between, has literally to be seen to be believed. I would recommend to anyone that, leaving aside the European and World Championships and the Olympic Games, if they want to watch show jumping at its very highest level, they should treat themselves to a trip to a World Cup final. It really is indoor show jumping at its highest level.

On paper this all sounds very pleasant for riders, which of course it is, provided you have capable horses and as long as they are qualified to get into the show which you want to go to. Show jumping is in this country as strong as anywhere in the world. If you can win here, you can win anywhere. But the law of supply and demand rules that major show organisers have continually to try to find the fairest way of attempting to get a quart into a pint pot.

The World Cup series, which is a law unto itself and is not ruled from Britain, concerns so few riders from each nation that I need not discuss it here. But what of the other shows? The county circuit varies from show to show. Most accept entries on a first-come-first-served basis, others by invitation only or by taking a certain number from the BSJA computer list. There are so many good shows in the summer that if a rider misses out on one he can always say, 'Not to worry, I'll go to so and so instead' or give the horses a few days' break. It is not the end of the world.

But the three major indoor shows are very important, for various reasons. Firstly, of course, they are all televised nationwide, and televised packages of show jumping are also sold worldwide. Coverage is thus very big indeed, a fact which understandably is not overlooked by sponsors. Secondly, the level of prize money at our shows compares very favourably with, and in most cases outshines, other

European shows. Whereas on the Continent the first few days' competitions carry only moderate prize money, followed by one big lump in the Grand Prix, our shows carry the equivalent of a Grand Prix purse five nights on the trot. It is therefore very important for a rider to be at the shows where the big money can be won, not only to help make ends meet (which is difficult enough) but also to maintain a good place on the computer list so that he is again invited to the big shows when they come round. Prize money is converted to points by awarding 1 point for every £50 won. It is amazing by how many places a rider can move up the list through a really good show indoors. Some horses can, and do, click into gear and are in the shake-up nearly every night.

I think that the qualifications for shows are now very fair to everyone. There is a different formula for each of the 'big three'. The Horse of the Year Show is based, as it has always been, on prize money won during the year, which is how it should be for the leading horses of the year. One welcome innovation is the Sunday programme for horses who have won more than £2000 but not enough to qualify for the big competitions and to be ridden by riders not qualified for the whole week. The best four on aggregate over the two main competitions on that day are then allowed to stay for the rest of the show. The experiment worked well in its first two years because on both occasions all four of the qualifiers more than held their own against the best during the rest of the show.

The novice Grade Championships at Wembley are always fascinating. Many good horses have gone to the top after winning as novices at Wembley. The courses are quite strong these days and moderate horses have less chance of fluking a class than they did occasionally many years ago.

Olympia qualifications are largely based on international form: that is to say on Nations Cup appearances. The first ten riders are usually taken from the computer list, the remaining places going to riders who have represented Britain abroad that year. Places at Olympia are in shorter supply and therefore even more fought over than at the other big shows because Olympia, being a World Cup qualifier, draws most of the top riders on the European League. Every qualifier means a great deal in terms of winning points in order to get through to the highly lucrative and prestigious final.

Whereas the Horse of the Year Show is all about horses' qualifications, the Royal International, which now seems to have found a permanent venue at Birmingham's superb National Exhibition Centre, relies mainly on qualified riders. Again, the top ten are taken from the ranking list, the remaining places being given to riders who are out of the top ten but who have won the most points in Area International Trials throughout the country (the King George V Gold Cup and Queen Elizabeth II Cup have their own separate qualifications) This results in many AITs now attracting upwards of sixty to seventy starters, whereas a few years ago they had only half that number. An Area International Trial is a competition invented by the BSJA and designed to throw up possible international combinations for selection for British teams. There are minimum heights and widths on certain fences, and a reasonable sized water jump is obligatory, the idea being that the more capable international-type horse should win through. By and large, the system works pretty well.

One series of international shows which is open to everyone is Hickstead. That is the way Douglas Bunn likes to run his shows, and he is to be commended for his attitude. But his All England Jumping Course really has only its jumping programme to worry about and time is not so much at a premium when there are just two main classes each day, with a supporting programme which can revolve around them.

Team Selection
British teams are selected by an international subordinate committee which as well as including members of the executive is now strengthened by the presence of two or three senior international riders who are, of course, best qualified to know each horse's capabilities and recent form. For fairness in selection, this can only be a good thing. Again, it is very hard to please everyone, but decisions on committees are not taken lightly and each member does his or her utmost to see that justice is done. I will never forget discussing, literally for hours, which of two riders was to make up the fifth place in the Los Angeles Olympic team.

In England we have the same recurring problem: not in our case who to send but more often who to leave out. Of course, unlike in other countries the great majority of our top riders turned – or were turned – professional quite some time ago. This left us at a distinct disadvantage in the Olympic Games, where many riders who are patently just as gainfully employed in show jumping as the professionals still ride as amateurs. However, this situation should now be sorted out, since professionals will be able to revert to being amateurs (on a once-only basis) for the Olympics, and these days very few riders turn professional in the first place.

There is a popular misconception that to jump a Nations Cup or, even more, an Olympic course, a horse merely has to have tremendous scope and at the same time be brave enough to use it. That is over-simplyfing things. It is not enough merely to come out at the other end. Nations Cups and Olympic medals are not won by careless freaks who could jump anything but who are not too worried if a few poles get in the way. Over the years, results have shown that top-class ability plus a great deal of care are needed. The horse who shines through is usually a top money-winner anyway.

CHAPTER 11

Running Your Own Yard

There are many contributory factors which go towards the
achievement of optimum performance from a show
jumper. One thing which cannot be underestimated is the
value of a good environment: like human beings, horses
who are happy at home are more likely to be successful in
their job. Likewise, if a yard is designed for maximum
efficiency, with due regard for time and motion study and
labour-saving techniques, then the staff seem to stay
longer and to be more agreeable, too. I have been fortunate
with my present yard in that the entire place has been built
from scratch, facilities being added as the need arose. The
whole unit now works very well.

The Tack Room
Time and motion study is an important aspect of running a
yard. When you take into consideration the amount of
fetching and carrying, toing and froing, all day and
everyday, it follows that the tack room needs to be situated
where it is easily accessible to the stables. In a perfect
world, for security reasons it would also be close to the
house: but whatever its location, nowadays when saddlery
thefts are so common, the tack room needs to be very
securely locked, and to have barred windows. Even if your
tack is insured, do not count on getting paid by the insurers
unless your security is up to standard.

As far as fittings are concerned, plenty of saddle and
bridle hooks are a must, as well as ample space for storage
of rugs, blankets, and so on. I try to have space for each
horse's own rugs, boots, etc, and then stack away on higher
shelves the least used rugs and extra blankets. When you
have masses of tack to clean, a sink and hot water heater on
site are preferable. A saddle horse, for cleaning saddles on,
and a bridle hook, are also essential. In winter I always
keep the room warm to prevent tack from becoming damp
and mouldy, though this will not happen if it is cleaned
regularly.

I have a show bridle for each competition horse in the
yard, as well as a pool of working bridles for exercising, or

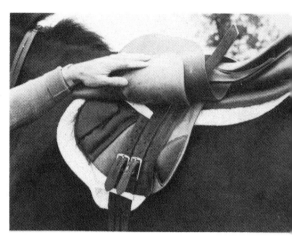

In common with most riders, I like everything about my saddles to be identical and to feel the same on each horse. The set-up in this picture is the one that I've found works best. The heavyish Continental-mode saddle can be a bit hard on the horse's back, and in most cases I use a short foam rubber backpad on top of a shaped or square quilted numnah. The stirrups all have the same rubber treads and are the same width; buffalo leathers seem to wear as well as most.

I use this particular type of saddle because it sits the rider in an ideal position, right in the middle of the horse, with ample support from the knee and thigh rolls.

one to each horse, depending upon how many are in. When the horses go out for a hack or out in the fields on healthy exercise, they work in a simple snaffle bridle; but when they are being worked seriously on the flat, or jumping, all the horses wear their show bridles. My standard exercise bridle would be fitted with a long running martingale, cavesson noseband and some form of snaffle.

It is worth cultivating a few general golden rules where the tack room is concerned. Since it is a shared area it is everyone's responsibility to make sure that it is kept scrupulously clean and tidy at all times. When in use, tack should be cleaned every day, even if it is only given a quick rub over with a lick of saddle soap. Numnahs and summer sheets need washing regularly, but show rugs and jute stable rugs are best sent to the cleaners. Long experience has taught me to buy the best possible quality in any form of tack. Despite the initial expense, it is without doubt cheaper in the long run.

BOOTS

Overreach Boots
Prevention is always better than cure, and for years none of my horses ever jumped a fence without the protection of overreach boots. But I have come to the conclusion that

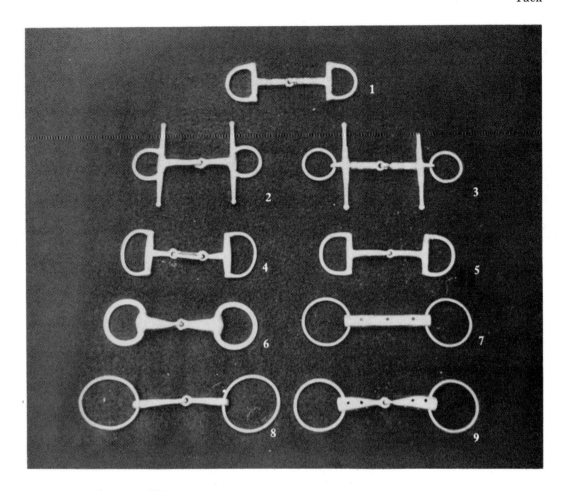

A small selection from the bit box

1 A D-cheek copper roller snaffle. This is a favourite bit of mine; it has alternate copper and silver rollers and a lot of horses go nicely in it. If I ever feel the need for something just a little sharper than an eggbut snaffle, I most often try this one first. It's a very popular bit. Towerlands Anglezarke goes in one from time to time.

2 Eggbut Fulmer snaffle. This is a lovely soft bit for a young horse. The full cheeks certainly help with direction. Ryan's Son always went in a Fulmer snaffle.

3 Copper roller Fulmer snaffle. An interesting variation, just a bit sharper than the plain snaffle, this time with a loose ring.

4 A Dr Bristol. Again, quite popular, though quite honestly I've never really liked this bit and rarely use one. A variation would be the similar French link snaffle.

5 Copper mouth eggbut snaffle. One or two horses go very well in this. I think the theory is that the copper mouth helps horses to salivate, and consequently become a little bit softer in the mouth.

6 Hollow mouth eggbut snaffle. A very soft, kind bit, which is both light and comfortable for a nicely mouthed horse.

7 Straight-bar fluted snaffle. Just like a piece of pipe with holes in it, and I suppose a bit gimicky, but handy to have in the bit box for the odd occasion.

8 German snaffle, loose ring.

9 Loose-ring fluted jointed snaffle. I quite like this one. Horses tend not to grab at it and one or two have been a lot lighter to ride in this.

The alum bridle. The odd horse can have a tendency to be chafed by the bit or even develop a small cut in the corner of the mouth. The alum bit is marvellous for repairing the damage, even when used overnight for a competition next day. It's just an ordinary snaffle, padded with gauze and cotton wool, and soaked in a solution of warm water and alum crystals. Alum is easily obtainable from most chemists and its healing properties are quite remarkable. Corunna Bay used to wear this outfit a lot as he had a soft mouth but pulled like a train, and his mouth split easily (hence his usual appearance in a hackamore). On show days in between feeds and after his last feed and hay, he'd quite happily stand in this bridle and was always ready to go again next day. It needs to be soaked often to keep it moist. The transformation on a sore mouth will be almost instantly apparent as the alum takes the redness and soreness away.

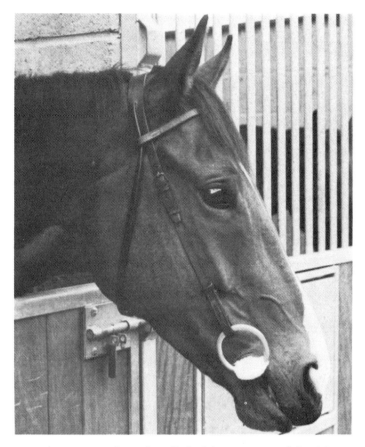

some horses are just that little bit more careful without boots than they are with them, so now I only use them on horses whom I really rate and those who have a tendency to overreach. There are all sorts of boots on the market, but I have found Pariani to be the best from the point of view of wear and tear. With their various sizes, they also seem to fit most horses well.

Tendon Boots
Again, prevention is best, and no horse in my yard ever goes out on exercise, and certainly never jumps, without a pair of protective tendon boots. More often than not I use the open-fronted ones – it is just the back of the tendon which is protected. It is all too easy for a horse to strike himself from behind when working or jumping, and a damaged tendon can mean a lengthy lay-off, or worse.

Brushing Boots
Whether or not you use brushing boots really depends on the horse concerned. If he brushes, he needs protecting from himself.

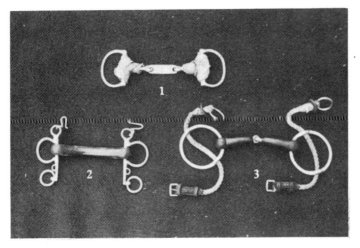

Fetlock Boots

A favourite boot of mine is one that fits just around the fetlock joint itself and is very light. An alternative could be a square of felt folded over a tape and tied on the outside of the joint. This is known as a Yorkshire boot.

BANDAGES

Stable Bandages

There are many types of stable bandage on the market, all in varying price ranges. I tend to use Velcro fastenings more than tapes as there is less likelihood of their being fastened too tightly and so damaging a tendon. With stable bandages I quite often use squares of old Whitney blankets as padding underneath, or white Fibretac which, although expensive to buy initially, lasts and washes well. Gamgee does not last very long and is too expensive for constant replacing – unless of course a horse needs a wound covering or a cold water bandage. Although stable bandages lend support to tired legs, they should never be fitted so tightly that they restrict circulation.

Travelling Bandages

Travelling bandages are used in the same way as stable bandages. There are horses who need protection for their heels, and some people actually travel their horses in overreach boots. Many horses knock their hocks in the lorry through sitting back against the wall. I guard against this by fitting a large piece of sponge under the bandages and up to the point of the hock. I do not use knee boots for travelling. They certainly offer a bit more protection for horses facing front or back, but since my horses always travel diagonally they do not need them.

However, I do use knee boots for road exercise: a horse

1 Corunna Bay went in this one quite a bit, hence the chamois leather. He would work well in it at home on the flat but always ran away in the ring, where he went either in a hackamore or the rope gag below. The Dr Bristol is quite a strong bit and is difficult for the horse to get hold of. Although this bit is padded on both sides, it's sometimes necessary, in the case of a horse who's more ignorant to one side or the other, just to pad one side. You can then ring the changes by padding only the good side, making it harder and more severe on the other.

2 Vulcanite Pelham. I'm not a great fan of curb chains, except in the case of the double bridle, but I certainly wouldn't be against a vulcanite Pelham for a strongish horse. With a pair of Ds for the cheeks, and a rubber-guarded curb chain, this bit can be firm, yet soft at the same time, and if a horse takes to it he'll go really sweetly in it. Flying Wild went in one for several seasons.

3 The rope gag can be a useful bit for a strong, ignorant horse, and can be very useful short term. The vulcanite mouth is quite soft really, and I like the rope sides because they run very easily.

who goes down on his knees on the road can do himself a lot of damage. Knee boots are a simple form of protection.

Exercise Bandages

Exercise bandages are widely used by show jumpers to support tired tendons. But for a sound horse, too, a little extra support on very hard or very soft ground certainly cannot do any harm, and will save some wear and tear.

Tail Bandages

Tail bandages are a must for travelling but, again, be careful not to tie tapes too tightly. I also use a tail guard over the top of the bandage. From a grooming point of view, standing a horse in a tail bandage for an hour or two will keep a pulled tail tidy and laid flat.

First Aid Kit

I only keep basic items in my first aid kit: bandages, Gamgee, cotton wool, disinfectant, wound powder, chloromycetin spray, wound cream, liniment, Animalintex, Stockholm tar, Epsom salts, common salt and Amorican paste or powder (for the undesirable but inevitable lumpy knee or capped hock) – everything in fact that is needed to cope with normal everyday ailments, nicks, cuts and bruises.

RUGS

Stable Rug

The traditional stable rug is made of jute and lined with wool, though nowadays rugs made of lighweight modern fabrics are becoming more popular, not least because they are machine-washable. Rollers can be of jute or leather, and though the leather kind are more expensive they will, if cared for, last much longer. Rugs made of quilted nylon material with a cotton or nylon lining are light and very warm. Some come with their own matching roller, but in my experience they are not satisfactory as, being nylon, they do not prevent rugs from slipping.

In winter, particularly if he is clipped, a horse will need additional protection. I use a Witney blanket under a jute rug, with an old summer sheet under the blanket next to the skin (it is so much easier to clean a sheet than a blanket) and an anti-cast roller, with or without a breastplate according to the individual horse. Three layers will keep most horses warm, though in extremely cold weather I might add a quarter sheet between the blanket and the jute rug to give added warmth over the loins.

188

To keep the horse comfortable and to minimise pressure on his back, the roller must be well padded and should be placed over a foam or folded blanket pad. Like the modern New Zealand rugs, some new-style stable rugs require no roller at all, in which case this problem is eliminated altogether.

Some horses develop the annoying (and expensive) habit of removing and/or chewing their rugs and may need to wear a headcollar fitted with a bib. In theory this should prevent them from being able to grasp the rugs with their teeth, although in practice it is not always so. I remember a horse called Gimple who regularly removed his rugs and put them over the stable door, though not before he had shredded them. He could even get out of a tightly fitted breastplate and roller – I never did find out how. I fitted a plastic bib shaped like a scoop, to his headcollar, but this merely gave rise to another problem. Every night, at the end of evening stables, when the yard was spotless and the brooms put away, he would appear at his door with a scoopful of shavings and proceed to throw them over the yard. This went on until the bib was removed. I finally gave up putting rugs on him and eventually he grew out of the chewing habit.

Show Rug

Heavy woollen show or day rugs look smart and keep a horse warm while he is travelling and standing at the ringside. If your pocket can bear the strain, the horse can have matching roller, tail guard, knee boots and hock boots.

Waterproof Rug

A waterproof rug is invaluable for use at shows. The ones with detachable hoods are ideal. Although it is an expensive item it will last for many years if looked after. A soaked, cold, miserable horse is not likely to want to give of his best when competing, so it is money well spent. Sunorra hated the rain (she did not like extreme heat either) and would always turn herself round to avoid it.

New Zealand Rug

A New Zealand rug is designed to provide both warmth and protection from the rain and is essential for a horse who spends some of his time at grass. As with other items of horse clothing, it undoubtedly pays to buy the very best that you can afford. Of the two basic types – one is fitted with a sewn-on surcingle, the other requires no surcingle at all – I prefer the latter. It is cut and shaped to the body of the horse, fits snugly round the neck and is much deeper than the other type. This extra depth not only gives added warmth but also helps to keep the rug in place. It is fitted with hind leg straps which loop around each other and fasten on the same side to which they are attached. The great advantage of this type of rug, in addition to the extra warmth it provides, is the lack of pressure on the horse's back from a surcingle. The other style of rug is held in place by the surcingle plus two straps, each one of which crosses between the hind legs and is secured to a metal ring on the opposite bottom corner of the rug.

With all New Zealand rugs, a close, secure fit is essential, and care must be taken when fastening buckles and straps. Always keep an eye on a horse turned out in a rug. If it slips it can cause chafing and may even result in a horse taking fright and injuring himself.

Exercise Rug

In cold weather a clipped horse not in strong work may need a light woollen exercise rug (known in the racing world as a 'paddock sheet'). Always use a fillet string under the tail to prevent the rug from flapping about.

Sweat Rug

An essential item for going to shows is a sweat rug, designed to prevent a horse catching a chill after he has been in hard work. It helps him to cool down without losing too much body heat. A sweat rug may be used on its own or, on colder days, underneath a jute rug, which should be put on upside down, to prevent the lining from becoming damp with sweat, and should have the front turned back. Rugs made of nylon are not suitable for use in this way, since they do not breathe well, and thus retain moisture. (A rug which does allow the skin to breathe is the heavy Glentona.)

Summer Sheet

A lighweight cotton sheet with a front fastening is useful for travelling to shows in the summer. In hot weather it will keep the sun off the horse's back, prevent his coat from standing up, and give protection from flies. As already mentioned, a summer sheet – perhaps one that has seen better days – also makes a useful undersheet for the stabled horse. It adds a little extra warmth and, unlike heavy blankets and rugs, is easy to wash and dry.

The Feed Room and Feeding

Like the tack room, the feed room should also be centrally

situated in relation to the stables. For storage I use strong galvanized metal bins raised an inch or two off the floor on wooden battens to prevent damp from creeping underneath. My feed room is on two levels, all the bins, buckets and mucking out tools being on ground level, with a loft above for the storage of extra corn, bags of chaff, jump stands and poles, etc. Corn is best bought fresh and not stored for too long. It soon loses some of its feed value and also becomes unappetising or even a bit musty. In the main I feed chaff, bran, oats, coarse horse mixture and sugar beet pulp. Chaff bulks the feeds up well and helps to get horses burly without their being corned up to the eyeballs. Every month or two I have a mill/mix firm come with a lorry and chop up my own mixture: two-thirds good hay, one-third good clean straw. Mixed as it is with molasses, and chopped finely, it helps to make up a really appetising feed. I now find that I really would not be satisfied to feed horses without it.

Modern-day know-how in the Thoroughbred world dictates that bran, broad or otherwise, has no food value and is best not used at all. Old habits die hard and I still use perhaps a double handful or a little less in each feed. I give an Epsom salts bran mash every other week or so to clear the horses' systems.

Oats must be of exceptionally good quality, just broken rather than squashed flat, and fed as freshly milled as possible. Some horses can tolerate oating up, others cannot take oats at all. That again is down to the individual and is a question of trial and error.

Most reputable firms these days produce an excellent coarse horse mixture which seems to have just about everything in it and is certainly very palatable. Although it is expensive, it is high in protein and can be fed in reasonably small quantities along with the bran, chaff and sugar beet pulp. I feed a double handful or so of the latter at each feed to dampen it and also as an appetiser. I feed morning and night, with ad lib hay for most of the novices. The graded horses, however, are fed very much as individuals where both corn and hay are concerned. Horses are fussy feeders, so feed them only good quality hay and do not let them waste it by treading it into their beds. Where bad hay is concerned, not only is the food value almost negligible but horses will also waste almost as much as they eat.

In winter I like to feed a boiled feed several times a week: either a linseed gruel or boiled barley and linseed mixed. A quicker boil in terms of cooking time is plain boiled bruised oats which turn out a bit like porridge but, importantly, lose their heating properties and really help to put weight on. A boil like this only takes about an hour, as opposed to most of the day in the case of whole grain.

Like the tack room, the feed room should be kept scrupulously clean. Feed buckets should be washed out after every feed, and all water drinkers/buckets should also be kept spotlessly clean. Every horse needs a constant supply of clean, fresh water.

Hay

Well-made, first or second year seed hay is the best for horses in work, but well-made, clean meadow hay may have good herbage and a nice nose to it, and in some cases can be better value than badly made seed hay.

I now feed hay to all my horses from low-level mangers. Since flat work is geared towards lowering the horse's head, it seems pointless to me to let a horse spend upwards of twelve hours a day nibbling hay from a net or rack with his nose higher than his ears. Some people feed hay from the box floor but I think this is wasteful as the hay gets trodden into the bed. This feeding method can also cause damage to rugs, through the horses' chest bursting out of the front buckles. What you lose in wasted hay and rug repairs soon pays for the sort of low level hay mangers illustrated on page 203.

I feed very little in the way of additives, since I believe that if the hard feed and hay are of sufficiently good quality, there should be no reason to add anything. I do, however, have a lump of rock salt in every manger.

BEDDING

Straw

I use all sorts of straw – wheat, barley and oat. I buy it from my neighbouring farmer and take it as it comes, as long as it is good. The greater part is barley. I like straw. It is far more economical than any other form of bedding and is much easier to dispose of. Many stables have a contract with a local mushroom farm, who come and collect the whole muck heap at regular intervals.

In the winter I muck out straight into the cattle pens. The cattle browse through it and eat what hay or clean straw there is and then tread down the rest, making excellent muck which goes on to the land in the spring or autumn. In summer I muck out on to the muck heap in the field behind the stables. In time it rots down and, again, goes on the land.

Shavings
There is little doubt that shavings are more expensive than straw, but even so they can be reasonably economical to use if boxes are mucked out carefully. The one big problem with shavings is that they are more difficult to dispose of and in most cases have to be burned. I probably use shavings in two or three boxes out of ten, simply because some horses have an allergy to the dust in straw or eat their beds and have to be dieted.

Although I use straw and shavings, according to the individual horse, I really prefer a straw bed. I always put down a good thick base and bank the bed well up the walls, as shown here.

Again, as with straw, this shavings bed has a good thick bottom to it and is well banked up the walls. Some jumpers would simply become too heavy if bedded on straw, and too thick in the wind from the dust.

There's no way that you could describe these feet as a pair but believe me they do belong to the same horse. The foot on the right is normal and well shaped; it's perhaps a bit long in the toe, but then it's obviously about ready for the blacksmith. The one on the left is a lot smaller, with less body and a concave outer wall. This horse was a very sound goer and would not necessarily go lame because of his feet. But he'd have to be a pretty talented performer for me to buy him because if he missed as a jumper, and had to be sold on, a vet might just reject him. This particular horse's feet did improve a lot after a period of skilful attention from my black-smiths, David and John Coles.

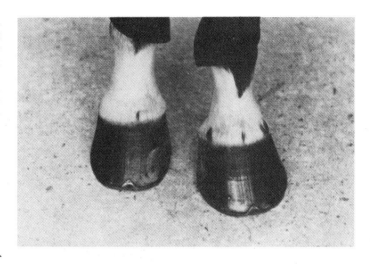

Other Types of Bedding

The other alternative beddings are paper and peat. Since I have never in fact used either I am in no position to judge, but I have never seen the need to try, because straw and shavings have always served me adequately.

The Vet

A good local vet is essential. Not only must he be close to hand in case of emergencies, he must also specialise in large animals, with at least a leaning towards horses. Do not call out the vet unnecessarily – it is expensive as well as a waste of his time – but do call him promptly in a crisis. In an emergency every second is critical.

The Blacksmith

Again, the local one may be the best. When moving to a new part of the country, ask a few reliable horsey people in that area to recommend someone. Try to avoid becoming attached to a blacksmith who has more temperament than talent – some think that they are God's gift to the horse world. Make sure that they will come out when you want them.

Having found the right man, allow him free rein over your horses. I let the blacksmith decide when a horse needs new shoes or a set of removes, and a good man can be a great asset with a horse who has bad feet and needs specialised attention. The well-used old saying 'no foot, no horse' seems to apply even more to show jumpers than it does to anything else.

Turning the Horse Out to Graze

Whenever possible in spring, summer and autumn I let my

Fit horses, who are stabled most of the time, are liable to fight when turned out for breaks in the day and may cause each other serious injury. I turn mine out individually in threes, in the three nursery paddocks or playpens. The horses are company for each other and the size of the paddocks enables them to canter round without getting up too much speed. They soon settle down and pick at a bit of grass and thoroughly enjoy themselves on a nice day. I never use the playpens in winter or in a very wet period because the horses cut them up too much. Although I had to grit my teeth when writing out the cheque for the pens, I've since found them so useful that it was definitely money well spent. In the foreground you can see that the rails are attached to either side of the posts: this gives horses on both sides of the fence a smooth line to run along so that they don't knock either shoulders or hips on them. Wicket gates from pen to pen are totally adequate and work better in practice than full-sized gates. Towards the top right-hand side of the photograph, between the big thorn bush and the hedge, is a set of slip rails. These are provided into and out of every paddock to allow a tractor through for harrowing and rolling, for topping the grass occasionally or, once a year, to let in the mechanical trimmer to do the hedge.

horses out to graze for an hour or two. They go out either in pairs in the large paddocks or singly in the nursery paddocks, where they have a chance to relax and roll freely. They are always happier in stables and much more level headed to ride if allowed out as often as possible. On average, each horse has around one hour's exercise each day, so unless he has a chance to go out in the paddocks he spends the next twenty-three hours shut in – which does not help an animal's mentality in any way. In winter I turn

The only double post and railing which I have separates the jumping paddock from its neighbouring field, but finance permitting I'd fence the whole place in this way. It's annoying to see horses arguing and sometimes fighting from opposite sides of a fence and is also very damaging to the railings. A little extra money spent on buying rails which have been pressure treated with creosote is money well spent. My fencing is remarkably chew-free – the railings in this photograph are more than five years old but are still as good as new. Although horses tend to stand under the two ash trees pictured here, they are far enough away from their neighbours to prevent any trouble. In a jumping yard the odd horse will often pop out of one field into another but I haven't yet had a horse take on this particular bit of fencing.

them out in the indoor school to let off steam every so often, but again only singly, because fit, fresh horses with shoes on tend to do each other far too much grievous bodily harm if left to their own devices.

It is usually not too difficult to find two geldings who will agree, and those two can always be paired up to go out to graze in one of the bigger fields. Some horses are absolute villains to others, and can only be turned out singly. Even then, care should be taken, because a single horse in a paddock may be inclined to jump out. I always have the services of my wife Clare's first pony, who now potters about in retirement at the age of thirty but more than earns her keep by providing company for the horses.

Give a little thought to the question of how long a horse should be allowed to graze. In spring and early summer, when the grass is at its best, a stuffy horse can put on too much weight too quickly if allowed to gorge himself. On the other hand, the leaner individual will benefit from a much longer time, and will be all the better for being more robust.

Rest Days

In mid-season there are times when days off are difficult to
fit in, but usually my horses have a rest day (or two) after a
weekend of shows, to let them relax and unwind and
generally recharge their batteries ready to go again. These
periods of relaxation are especially important for novices,
who will soon fall out with the job if it is all work and no
play. If the weather is really good, I quite often let the
novices have a few days – even nights, too – out at grass,
and the graded horses also benefit from afternoons spent in
the field. On very wet or cold days I have the benefit of the
indoor school for playtime, either singly or in trustworthy
pairs.

If the staff have the day off, and the horses have had a
bran mash the evening before, it does no harm for them all
to stand in for a day on the odd occasion; horses, too, need
to have a peaceful day now and again, away from human
beings. On such days I either have a skeleton staff in or do
them myself. It is an excellent way of getting to know one's
horses even better. In some ways this arrangement is more
convenient. If all the staff have the same day off, it does get
it over and done with in one shot and leaves only one day in
the week disturbed. Some people may find it hard to
believe, but at Christmas I really enjoy doing all the horses
myself. Having sent all the staff home for a few days, Clare
looks after the house and I look after the horses, and I
really do find that it is an excellent way of becoming aware
of odd little details about the running of the yard, and
about some of the horses themselves, which could
otherwise go unnoticed.

Fit, Fat or Frail

Horses tend to arrive in a yard in various states of physical
condition. When getting any horse fit for competition the
rider must have a good idea in his mind of just how much
condition he wants to have on his animal. Some horses are
born to do themselves well – they are good poor man's
horses because they spend all their lives looking sleek and
fat however much an owner tries to diet them. The other
end of the scale are the narrow, greyhound types, who
seem to stay that way no matter how much food they
consume. To do himself justice in competition, a horse
should not be overfat. The burly, roly-poly look so often
seen in the show ring has no place in show jumping.
Competing and training put enough wear and tear on a
horse's feet and limbs without his carrying a hundred-
weight too much condition.

The overfat horse, however, is the easier type to come to

terms with. In most cases he simply needs a strict diet, a small ration of hay and a bed of shavings, coupled with an intelligent work programme, for his shape to change rapidly for the better. The frail, weedy horse's condition takes very much longer to rectify. As with most human beings, the first place in which a horse gains weight is around his middle. From there it spreads to his backside, then to the back and loins and lastly the neck, which is why a light-framed, poorly fleshed horse appears to have such a scrawny neck. It is always difficult to get this type to put on weight in the right place: that is, along his top line. The only way such a horse will develop muscle where it matters is by quite literally putting on a tremendous amount of weight and being worked in a good shape and outline over a considerable amount of time by a skilful person. Ultimately, the horse will put on weight where it matters.

To withstand the rigours of training and travelling, a horse needs to be big and well in himself, as well as trained hard and tight. Jumpers do not need to be as fit as racehorses, but a soft, stuffy, overweight animal certainly needs training along the same lines.

Programme for the Working Day
Work in my yard usually starts at seven o'clock on normal working days: earlier if the weather is very hot. At such times of year I like to have the work programme finished by mid- to late morning, after which all the staff can have a couple of hours off from lunchtime to mid-afternoon. Most of the time I enjoy feeding the horses myself. Feeding is such a personal thing, and I am a great believer in the old saying 'It's the eye of the man that fattens the horse'. I try to have all the mucking out finished and everywhere swept up by 8.30a.m. so that the first horses can pull out for work immediately after breakfast, by around 9 o'clock. Sometimes Clare and I ride while the girls are mucking out, especially if there are a lot of horses to work or we have other things to do later in the day. If all the exercising is done in the morning, the horses can have an hour or two out in the paddocks up to lunchtime or perhaps be led out to have some grass in the afternoon. I like to get the horses out of their boxes at least twice a day, especially if they are in the indoor yard and do not have a room with a view. Happy horses are far easier to train, to ride and to look after than horses who are treated like machines and shut up in their boxes for twenty-three hours a day.

This regime leaves the afternoon free for the girls to do all the grooming and tack cleaning, and leaves me free to do other jobs. I normally feed at around five to five-thirty. I

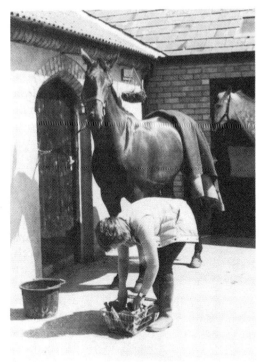

Every evening Clare and I write up a horses' work list for the following morning. When we have a fair number of horses in, in work, things become a bit chaotic if we don't have a programme to work to. Here, we appear to be discussing who is worked next. I don't remember this photograph being taken, but judging by the sheepskin coats and gloves it must have been in the dead of winter.

Doing a horse over late on a summer afternoon. I'd only tie up a quiet horse out on the yard. The girl here has been sensible enough to tie the rope through a loop of string in case the horse runs back, and is also keeping a rug over his hindquarters while she does his front half to save him from getting chilled.

do not like to keep staff hanging about on normal working days. Like horses, they need to be kept sweet, too, and some show days can be very long-drawn-out affairs.

Clipping

There are no hard and fast rules on clipping a show jumper. In a hot summer I keep most of my horses clipped out throughout the season, especially the graded ones, who are more likely to be in strenuous work. They can be washed down easily, dried off quickly and must feel a lot cleaner, fitter and more comfortable. With a nice quality horse I prefer to leave the hair on the legs; it keeps the legs warm, and some horses do look freaks with their legs taken out. Conversely, it may suit the more common horse to have the legs clipped right out since they can look equally comical if they are not.

A good clip for winter is the blanket clip, or even a

version of the old trace clip, where some of the neck is left on. A cold horse will never do well. Horses thrive on warmth, and I only clip a horse right out if it is absolutely necessary, and in winter only as a last resort.

There are plenty of clippers on the market now. The busy yard needs at least two sets with a cooling system for prolonged use. In addition, a small set of quiet dog clippers is a great help with tickly bits and difficult heads.

Trimming

A horse's whole appearance can be spoiled by a badly managed mane and tail. A horse's mane should be neatly pulled so that it will lie over and stay on the correct side. Snip out a path over the poll just wide enough for the bridle, but do not let a horse become 'half hogged' through careless clipping here. Similarly, with the withers, do not trim off the hair too far up the neck, otherwise the horse will be made to look short-necked through having only half a mane.

Whiskers and heels can be trimmed very easily with little clippers. Of if a horse is very fidgety and headshy, whiskers can be neatly trimmed by wetting the nose and running a disposable razor gently over the hairs. Tails look best either pulled or left full. After a tail has been pulled it needs only the slightest attention once a week or so to remove stray hairs. Some horses, understandably, do not like having their tails pulled, and mine most often have theirs pulled over a stable door. Some horses look better with a full (unpulled) tail, others with a plaited tail. It is largely a matter of preference, and as long as it looks tidy it is a question of owner's choice.

Plaiting

As a general rule, I decide to plait or not to plait according to the grade of the horse or the calibre of the show. A neatly pulled mane, which lies over to one side, looks tidy and workmanlike. Most show jumping grooms use rubber bands for quickness when plaiting, and gone are the days of seven plaits only. Nowadays anything from twelve to twenty is normal: though more than that, especially on a small horse, is a bit over the top.

The Stable Yard

My job involves a lot of travelling and visits to other people's premises both at home and abroad. I always find it interesting to compare stable yards and ancilliary buildings, and I try to pick up any new ideas which make sense to me.

Left: Swivel mangers are expensive but like so many other things they only have to be paid for once and are well worth the extra outlay. I have twelve Loddon stables in one line and wouldn't have believed how much time and effort is saved by not having to go into each individual box to feed each horse two or three times a day.

Above: Each manger is operated from the outside by a push-down, quick-release bolt. They're very positive and quick to operate. These particular mangers have a plug in the bottom which enables them to hold water if necessary or, more importantly, to be washed out regularly. When the horses have eaten their feeds someone walks down the whole line and turns the mangers round, leaving a flat wall on the inside. This is a good opportunity to check that all the horses have eaten up.

Basically, stabling falls into two types: (1) The traditional range of outside boxes, either converted from existing buildings, purpose-built from scratch, or purchased pre-fabricated and erected on site, and (2) internal boxes, erected inside a large building and sometimes called the American barn system. Since I have some of each, I am in a good position to make comparisons.

When I first moved into my present place in Warwickshire, apart from the house and a sound Dutch barn the only other building of value was a range of brick-build cowsheds. Those I quickly converted into seven loose-boxes, and I am well pleased with the results. Another building, attached to and running the full length of the indoor school, contains twelve stables plus ample storage space for hay and straw, show jumps, machinery, etc.

At first I contemplated building the internal stables from concrete blocks. But having been recommended to the purpose-built interior stables manufactured by Loddon Livestock Ltd, at Loddon near Norwich, I looked into the relative costs and eventually decided on the latter. I have never regretted the decision. Horses in general are destructive animals where stabling is concerned so that boxes have to be very well made to stand the hammering dished out to them. The Loddon boxes are very attractive to look at, with their hardwood and galvanised finish, and blend well with the concrete back and dividing walls. They have several useful features of their own which I have found first class to work with.

For preference I tend to use the internal boxes in winter. The outside boxes are fine, and indeed are warm enough

A pleasing sight in the outdoor yard: horses all done up for the night, rugs all in order, yard swept and, by the look of it, just the feeding to do. I tend to use the outside yard more for the jumpers who are travelling in the summer, as they're in stables for a long time; they can look out from these boxes across open country. I always use kick-over bolts for the lower fasteners on the doors, which save a lot of bending down, and self-fastening spring-loaded bolts on the top. These, again, are labour saving, though there is one snag: I have them on the top doors, too, and if the latter are not fastened back to the wall, a gust of wind can slam them and shut someone in the stable. This is an interesting line of horses. On the left is old Rough and Tumble, who was second and third in the Grand National when trained by Fred Winter and ridden by John Francome. The middle three are part of the team of six which I took over from the late Caroline Bradley following her untimely death in 1983. The white-faced mare Granita never quite made it, but the grey in the centre certainly did. His name is Next Milton. The brown horse next to him is Rubber Ball, who won all sorts of classes and was a top score specialist, and on the right is dear old Sunorra, who always campaigned from her big box in the corner.

These top bolts work very well. They're positive, accurate, hard wearing and totally chew-proof. If a horse plays with his bolt and opens doors, as so many do, these are easy enough to lock by putting a snap catch through the eyelets in front of the bolt. Stable doors need to be made of very hard wood or be protected with metal all over the front, otherwise they'll be severely chewed in next to no time.

I'm very much in favour of these low-level hay mangers. They're hard wearing and have a grid at the bottom to let the dust and seeds fall through into the bed. The horses really do use them and don't drag hay all over the bed. To me the real beauty of them is that horses stand there eating for many hours with their heads in the right place.

Every yard of any size needs a part-time handyman on a regular basis, and I've been lucky indeed to have had the help of Percy Wilcox since I moved to Warwickshire in 1981. There are always so many odd jobs to do around the place, if only on repairs after destructive horses. Incidentally, Percy doesn't always drive the dumper around with his eyes closed, nor is he camera shy, but he's certainly giving a good impression of both in this shot!

Concrete is expensive but indispensible. I don't think that wide expanses of concrete necessarily detract from a yard although I do sometimes feel that acres of block-work, such as I have on the end of my indoor school, tend to make a place look like a concrete jungle. I far prefer the bricks used in the tackroom on the left of the picture. They are certainly more expensive but I feel that they add a lot to the appearance of the place. The double doors to the building are very useful because they can be opened wide all day (at night, too, in hot weather) to allow free passage of air through the building. The corresponding doors at the other end of the building are high enough to admit tractors loaded with hay and straw, plus the feed lorry, which makes its appearance all too often.

for the horses, but from a working point of view the interior boxes are a favourite with everyone. Firstly, there is far less sweeping up to do, with no wind to blow hay, straw and shavings everywhere. Secondly, time and motion are kept to a minimum because all the bedding and foodstuffs are kept so near at hand. The best part of all is that no one has to work outside. When the weather is at its worst the horses go straight from their boxes into the school and never need to get wet or cold.

When to Sell, When to Keep

Having discussed in Chapter 1 how to set about buying a horse, perhaps this is the time to give a little thought to the question of when to sell him. All horses turn out differently from each other. Some improve rapidly, others not at all; a few go on to be stars, while others again may be worth even less after a year or two than when they started.

If you are fortunate enough to have come across a horse with a degree of talent, it is almost inevitable that at some stage someone will ask if the horse is for sale, or will possibly make an offer for him. Everyone's situation is different. Some people, as they say in Ireland, are sellers, others are not, and may become so attached to a horse (sometimes unwisely) that no amount of money or persuasion would make them sell. There is another wise old saying: 'It is better to sell and repent than keep and repent', and I suppose that in most cases that would be true. Timing is everything in business, and when selling a horse the clever part is knowing when to let go.

There are a number of things to be taken into consideration. If a rider has a horse who suits him ideally and, within reason, does not need the money, and if he can cope with the competition as the horse progresses up the ladder, then there is quite simply no reason for the horse to be sold. But in lots of other cases, when a horse improves dramatically, as does his value, then the rider must ask himself, 'Is it a viable proposition to keep this horse or would I be better cashing him in, buying another (or even two) and perhaps banking the change?' It is purely for the individual to decide. After all, he should know his own mind and situation better than anyone else.

There is another factor to consider. Sometimes the rate at which a horse's value rises, from his early novice days through to moving one or two steps up the ladder, can be greatly magnified if the horse evidently has the ability to go those extra, all-important steps. In these days of inflated, sometimes unrealistic, prices, a horse with talent can soon become worth an awful lot of money. The decision then has to be made: does his present rider want – or is he able to cope with – the pressure of competing at the next level? With horses, price governs everything, and in the long run it is a question of how much the horse is worth to his rider: he, after all, is the one who has to be best pleased.

Riding for Other People

The above comments obviously apply to the owner/rider. However, if a rider meets with any degree of success, it is almost inevitable that somewhere along the line he will be asked to ride a horse belonging to another owner. That is fine: few successful riders can make a business out of the sport with horses owned entirely by themselves, or their family, not only from the financial point of view, but also because good horses are so hard to come by that you really do have to get them where you find them. A talented rider who is winning classes should continue to do so, because he will attract the patronage of other owners and will therefore go on having his string replenished.

However, bearing in mind my earlier comments about when to sell and when to keep, the same situation is almost bound to recur – and can be a good deal more awkward – when someone else owns the horse. Riders accept horses on many different types of financial arrangement. Usually an agreement is made between owner and rider about running costs – livery, shoeing, travelling, vet's fees, entry fees – and a parallel agreement is arrived at about prize money. But I think the most important agreement of all is the one which decides what is to be done if and when the right customer comes along for the horse. There is no reason why that day should not be the best day of all for everyone concerned, as long as everyone knows, from the outset, where they stand. There must be a very clear understanding between owner and rider as to whether the horse is for sale at all, and if so at what figure and how it is to be shared.

I have been very fortunate throughout my riding career to have ridden for some very sound people. Even so, experience has taught me that it is wise to make a note of what has been decided upon or – far better still – to have a written agreement. Both parties then feel happy and it removes the strain from a rider, who might suddenly realise that, while he is sitting on a good horse which he does not want to lose, he has no control whatsoever over its owner. Many riders have found to their cost that they have spent an awful lot of time making a one-time unknown horse into a much hotter property, only to lose out because someone makes the owner an offer that he cannot refuse.

CHAPTER 12

Top Riders

There are so many enormously talented riders in the world that I find it difficult to compile a short-list of my favourites. I believe that the hallmark of a top rider is the ability to win at the highest level on a variety of horses over a period of years. All the following riders come into that category. I would not be so impressed with a rider who only achieved success on one outstanding horse. Each of the riders illustrated here is an out-and-out winner, with all the ingredients it takes to make a top competitor. They are all, in my opinion, always very watchable – something which is so important these days, when show jumpers have to compete with many other sports to gain the attention of the public.

Nick Skelton—St James
Since winning the Junior European Championship in 1975, Nick Skelton has become over the years one of the most competent all-round riders in the world. He's developed his own highly individual style, which works well for him, and is equally at home winning on a novice at a local show, at the gallop in a high quality speed class or in a major championship. His steely determination and ability win classes for him on horses who for many other riders would be impossible. His style suggests to me that he's doing 60mph when sitting still, and he's always exciting to watch.

Michael Whitaker—Next Warren Point

If I had to sum up Michael Whitaker (left) in one word it could only be 'winner'. My earliest recollection of Michael was when, just out of ponies, he used to gallop flat out from corners at Wembley to tackle combinations which he knew in his heart the diminutive Brother Scot was not really capable of jumping. That flair has never left him. He can ride just about anything and, almost without exception, win on it. His partnership with the talented but highly strung Next Warren Point has produced good results at the highest level, from the moment he won the first leg of the 1985 World Cup Final in Berlin, when the horse was little more than a novice, to being part of the runaway gold medal winning team in the 1985 European Championships in Dinard, where this photograph was taken. Exceptionally skilful and always exciting to watch, Michael is the sort of rider that show jumping badly needs.

Hugo Simon—Gladstone

Like Nick Skelton and Michael Whitaker, Hugo Simon (above) has that attention-catching style which pleases crowds and is always entertaining. But don't be misled by his extrovert antics in the saddle. He's technically very sound and understands the mechanics of the horse as well as anyone. Being small, he has to work extra hard to keep his big European horses in the shape in which he wants them, but when they get to a fence they really do explode for him. This photograph, so typical of Hugo, was taken when he won the gold medal in the 'substitute' Olympics, held in Rotterdam in 1980. One can almost feel the power with which Gladstone has left the ground. Hugo has given him every chance to jump this fence and is already working out his approach to the next.

LIBRARY
BISHOP BURTON COLLEGE
BEVERLEY HU17 8QG

John Whitaker—Next Milton

It's not a fluke that John Whitaker (left) has been at or around the top for many years. His quiet, adaptable style enables him to win on all kinds of horses, who go sweetly for him and really last. A rider who seems to attract good horses, John forged a great partnership with the superb Next Milton at just the right time, as the great Ryan's Son neared the end of his career. Milton is the sort of horse who can jump the biggest and widest fence with very little effort. At the time of writing still a young horse, he looks certain to have the best of his career in front of him.

Paul Schockemöhle—Deister

The record of Paul Schockemöhle and Deister (above) in the European Championships is nothing short of phenomenal, having won three on the trot, in 1981, 1983 and 1985. With those Championships, plus a host of Grand Prix wins and two Hickstead Derbies, the unorthodox Deister became a legend in his own lifetime.

In his own way Paul is equally remarkable. He turned to show jumping later in life than most and, although not a natural rider, through sheer determination and hard work made it to the very top. This is a typical shot of the great pair: Paul looks anything but comfortable and Deister is about to do his usual trick of twisting his hind legs to one side. But for all his idiosyncracies, the horse had immense scope, and generosity to match, and jumped an enormous amount of clear rounds.

Unfortunately Deister's career was cut short when at the age of 16 he pulled a check ligament at the 1987 European Championships, whereupon Paul retired him and immediately announced his own retirement from international riding.

Michael Matz—Chef

I suppose that Michael Matz (above) has to be regarded these days as one of the veterans of the United States team. He's certainly been winning competitions at the highest level for very many years. To my mind he has more of a leaning towards the European style than some American riders, but this photograph is typical of the skill and power with which he rides each horse. The German-bred Chef is making nothing of this fence but even so the competitive Michael is giving him every chance. Look at his ankle, which is still supporting the horse and holding him together even though he's already left the ground.

Gail Greenough—Mr T

Canada's Gail Greenough (right) literally took the world by storm when, as the outsider of four, she pulverised her three male opponents to win the individual gold medal in the 1986 World Championships in Aachen. Her simple, sympathetic, but highly effective style was appreciated by all four horses in the final, and there was no hint of fluke about her victory. This is a typical shot of her Hanoverian partner, Mr T, taken in the second round of the Team Championship. His flamboyant, free-going style is very apparent here and from the athletic way he uses his hindquarters, and tucks everything away behind him, there's no way that he's going to have many fences down behind. It'll be interesting to see if Gail can capitalise on her great win. With a talent like hers, and a personality to match, she should have every chance.

John Cottle—Isometric

Now based near Auckland, New Zealander John Cottle (above) had the foresight to spend several seasons touring England in the 1970s, where he more than held his own on the county and international circuit. Usually favouring the Thoroughbred type of horse, John has a lot of good form to his credit, and was always a danger in this country as he is in his own. This photograph suggests that there's a possibility of his taking the back rail with him, although Isometric doesn't appear to be sharing that view and is wisely looking where he's going.

Katie Monahan-Prudent—Special Envoy

Right: To my mind Katie Monahan's greatest strength is her ability to win big competitions on horses whom other top riders have discarded. Exceptionally powerful for a lady, she can ride any type of horse. This photograph is typical of her: a light contact, and powerful support from the leg. She gives the impression of being totally in control of almost any situation. Note the direction of her eyes. That fence is already as good as behind her. She's now working out the approach to the next. She's one of the most experienced of the great number of outstanding lady riders which the United States system produces.

Jeff McVean—Fürst Z

Jeff McVean (left) is typical of the tough brand of Australian riders who always make their presence felt on this side of the world. Jeff's style has changed dramatically over the years, through experience and observation of other top riders' techniques. He was always a winner right from the start, when his victories on the diminutive Claret included the prestigious King George V Gold Cup, to the present day when he now tours the major tournaments of Europe. Jeff is almost English these days, having been based at Stow on the Wold in Gloucestershire for several seasons past. Gone is the old acrobatic style of Claret's time. He's now as polished and pleasant to watch as any of his contemporaries.

Conrad Homfeld—Abdullah

One of the most outstanding present-day United States riders, Conrad Homfeld (above) has the distinction of having won the World Cup final twice, on Balbuco in Baltimore in 1980, and with Abdullah in Berlin in 1985. Winner of a team gold and individual silver medal in the 1984 Los Angeles Olympic Games, his form over the last decade bears the closest inspection. Exceptionally tall for a show jumping rider, he's of slim build but very powerful, and excels over the biggest courses on the very biggest occasions.

Robert Smith—Sanyo Bal Harbour

Over the past few years Robert Smith (above) has emerged as one of the most stylish and professional riders in Britain. Equally at home in a puissance or a hot speed class, he's capable of winning good competitions on virtually anything he rides. He's never quite had the horses which his outstanding talent deserves but, suitably mounted, would be capable of just about anything. A great competitor, blessed with a superb competition temperament, Robert has everything it takes to make a top rider.

Maurice Beatson—Jefferson Junior

A prolific class winner, Maurice Beatson (right) is probably the most popular rider in New Zealand. He has plenty of talent and is a tough, gritty competitor who wins competitions on horses which other riders would find difficult. Having won the New Zealand Horse of the Year title three times in the last four years, he has set his sights on bringing horses to Britain in 1989. The fence in this illustration is a good example of the superb set which Lester Jarden has put together for the New Zealand circuit. Lester photographed the most attractive fences at shows all over the world, and then simply built his own replicas. The results are really outstanding.

Peter Murphy—Blue Moon
After an outstanding career on ponies, Peter Murphy appears to be making the transition to horses with equal success. He's a great competitor, tremendously accurate, and has the ability, temperament and flair to make it to the very top. It'll be interesting to watch his career develop over the next few years.

INDEX

Note: [h] denotes the name of horses; numbers in italic refer to illustrations.

PICTURE CREDITS

Kit Houghton pages 11, 13, 14, 15, 16, 23 (bottom), 31, 32, 33,
35 (top), 36, 37, 39, 41, 43, 45, 47, 49, 51, 53, 54, 55, 57, 58, 60,
61, 62, 63, 64, 66, 67, 69 (top), 70, 71, 72, 75, 80, 81, 82, 83
(top), 84, 85, 87, 88, 89, 97, 105, 110, 114, 117, 119, 121, 123,
125, 127, 129, 130, 133, 135, 137, 149, 155, 156, 163, 167,
174 (bottom), 184, 185, 186, 187, 193 (right), 194, 195, 201,
203 (top right), 211, 213, 216, 217.   Riding Magazine 10, 12,
35 (bottom), 69 (bottom), 73, 77, 83 (bottom), 90, 91, 92, 93,
100, 109, 142, 193 (left), 199 (left), 202, 203 (top left).
Bob Langrish 199 (right), 207, 208, 209, 210, 212, 214, 215, 218,
220. Stuart Newsham 196, 203 (bottom). Werner Ernst 174 (top).